Implementing a
Body-Worn
Camera Program

Recommendations and Lessons Learned

Contents

Letter from the PERF Executive Director

T he recent emergence of body-worn cameras has already had an impact on policing, and this impact will only increase as more agencies adopt this technology. The decision to implement body-worn cameras should not be entered into lightly. Once an agency goes down the road of deploying body-worn cameras—and once the public comes to expect the availability of video records—it will become increasingly difficult to have second thoughts or to scale back a body-worn camera program.

A police department that deploys body-worn cameras is making a statement that it believes the actions of its officers are a matter of public record. By facing the challenges and expense of purchasing and implementing a body-worn camera system, developing policies, and training its officers in how to use the cameras, a department creates a reasonable expectation that members of the public and the news media will want to review the actions of officers. And with certain limited exceptions that this publication will discuss, body-worn camera video footage should be made available to the public upon request—not only because the videos are public records but also because doing so enables police departments to demonstrate transparency and openness in their interactions with members of the community.

Body-worn cameras can help improve the high-quality public service expected of police officers and promote the perceived legitimacy and sense of procedural justice that communities have about their police departments. Furthermore, departments that are already deploying body-worn cameras tell us that the presence of cameras often improves the performance of officers as well as the conduct of the community members who are recorded. This is an important advance in policing. And when officers or members of the public break the law or behave badly, body-worn cameras can create a public record that allows the entire community to see what really happened.

At the same time, the fact that both the public and the police increasingly feel the need to videotape every interaction can be seen both as a reflection of the times and as an unfortunate commentary on the state of police-community relationships in some jurisdictions. As a profession, policing has come too far in developing and strengthening relationships with its communities to allow encounters with the public to become officious and legalistic. Body-worn cameras can increase accountability, but police agencies also must find a way to preserve the informal and unique relationships between police officers and community members.

This publication, which documents extensive research and analysis by the Police Executive Research Forum (PERF), with support from the U.S. Department of Justice's Office of Community Oriented Policing Services (COPS Office), will demonstrate why police departments should not deploy body-worn cameras carelessly. Moreover, departments must anticipate a number of difficult questions— questions with no easy answers because they involve a careful balancing of competing legitimate interests, such as the public's interest in seeing body-worn camera footage versus the interests of crime victims who would prefer not to have their images disseminated to the world.

One of the most significant questions departments will face is how to identify which types of encounters with members of the community officers should record. This decision will have important consequences in terms of privacy, transparency, and police-community relationships. Although recording policies should provide officers with guidance, it is critical that policies also give officers a certain amount of discretion concerning when to turn their cameras on or off. This discretion is important because it recognizes that officers are professionals and because it allows flexibility in situations in which drawing a legalistic "bright line" rule is impossible.

For example, an officer at a crime scene may encounter a witness who would prefer not to be recorded. By using discretion, the officer can reach the best solution in balancing the evidentiary value of a recorded statement with the witness's reluctance to be recorded. The decision may hinge on the importance of what the witness is willing to say. Or perhaps the witness will agree to be recorded by audio but not video, so the officer can simply point the camera away from the witness. Or perhaps the witness will be willing to be recorded later, in a more private setting. By giving officers some discretion, they can balance the conflicting values. Without this discretion, body-worn cameras have the potential to damage important relationships that officers have built with members of the community. This discretion should not be limitless; instead, it should be guided by carefully crafted policies that set specific parameters for when officers may use discretion.

If police departments deploy body-worn cameras without well-designed policies, practices, and training of officers to back up the initiative, departments will inevitably find themselves caught in difficult public battles that will undermine public trust in the police rather than increasing community support for the police.

This publication is intended to serve as a guide to the thoughtful, careful considerations that police departments should undertake if they wish to adopt body-worn cameras.

Sincerely,

Chuck Wexler, Executive Director
Police Executive Research Forum

Letter from the COPS Office Director

Dear colleagues,

One of the most important issues currently facing law enforcement is how to leverage new technology to improve policing services. Whether using social media to engage the community, deploying new surveillance tools to identify suspects, or using data analysis to predict future crime, police agencies around the world are implementing new technology at an unprecedented pace.

Body-worn cameras, which an increasing number of law enforcement agencies are adopting, represent one new form of technology that is significantly affecting the field of policing. Law enforcement agencies are using body-worn cameras in various ways: to improve evidence collection, to strengthen officer performance and accountability, to enhance agency transparency, to document encounters between police and the public, and to investigate and resolve complaints and officer-involved incidents.

Although body-worn cameras can offer many benefits, they also raise serious questions about how technology is changing the relationship between police and the community. Body-worn cameras not only create concerns about the public's privacy rights but also can affect how officers relate to people in the community, the community's perception of the police, and expectations about how police agencies should share information with the public. Before agencies invest considerable time and money to deploy body-worn cameras, they must consider these and other important questions.

The COPS Office was pleased to partner with the Police Executive Research Forum (PERF) to support an extensive research project that explored the numerous policy and implementation questions surrounding body-worn cameras. In September 2013, the COPS Office and PERF hosted a conference in Washington, D.C., where more than 200 law enforcement officials, scholars, representatives from federal agencies, and other experts gathered to share their experiences with body-worn cameras. The discussions from this conference, along with interviews with more than 40 police executives and a review of existing body-worn camera policies, culminated in the recommendations set forth in this publication.

Implementing a Body-Worn Camera Program: Recommendations and Lessons Learned offers practical guidance as well as a comprehensive look at the issues that body-worn cameras raise. I hope you find that the wide range of perspectives, approaches, and strategies presented in this publication are useful, whether you are developing your own body-worn camera program or simply wish to learn more about the topic. The goal of the COPS Office and PERF is to ensure that law enforcement agencies have the best information possible as they explore this new technology; therefore, we encourage you to share this publication, as well as your own experiences, with other law enforcement practitioners.

Sincerely,

Ronald L. Davis, Director
Office of Community Oriented Policing Services

Acknowledgments

PERF would like to thank the U.S. Department of Justice's Office of Community Oriented Policing Services (COPS Office) for supporting this research into body-worn cameras. We are thankful to COPS Office Director Ronald Davis and Principal Deputy Director Joshua Ederheimer for recognizing the increasingly important role this technology plays for law enforcement agencies across the globe. We are also grateful to our program managers at the COPS Office, Helene Bushwick and Katherine McQuay, for their support and encouragement throughout the project.

We would also like to thank the law enforcement agencies that participated in our survey on body-worn cameras. Their thoughtful responses guided our research and the agenda for the executive session in Washington, D.C., in September 2013. We are also grateful to the more than 200 police chiefs, sheriffs, scholars, and other professionals who participated in our executive session (see appendix B for a list of participants). These leaders provided valuable information about their experiences with body-worn cameras and prompted an insightful discussion regarding the issues these cameras raise.

We are especially thankful for the more than 40 police executives who shared their body-worn camera policies with PERF and who participated in interviews with PERF staff. Their candid assessments of how this technology has impacted their agencies shaped the findings and recommendations found in this publication.

Finally, credit is due to PERF staff members who conducted the survey, prepared for and hosted the executive session, conducted interviews, and helped write and edit this publication, including Jessica Toliver, Lindsay Miller, Steve Yanda, and Craig Fischer.

Introduction

State of the field and policy analysis

Over the past decade, advances in the technologies used by law enforcement agencies have been accelerating at an extremely rapid pace. Many police executives are making decisions about whether to acquire technologies that did not exist when they began their careers—technologies like automated license plate readers, gunshot detection systems, facial recognition software, predictive analytics systems, communications systems that bring data to officers' laptops or handheld devices, GPS applications, and social media to investigate crimes and communicate with the public.

For many police executives, the biggest challenge is not deciding whether to adopt one particular technology but rather finding the right mix of technologies for a given jurisdiction based on its crime problems, funding levels, and other factors. Finding the best mix of technologies, however, must begin with a thorough understanding of each type of technology.

Police leaders who have deployed body-worn cameras[1] say there are many benefits associated with the devices. They note that body-worn cameras are useful for documenting evidence; officer training; preventing and resolving complaints brought by members of the public; and strengthening police transparency, performance, and accountability. In addition, given that police now operate in a world in which anyone with a cell phone camera can record video footage of a police encounter, body-worn cameras help police departments ensure events are also captured from an officer's perspective. Scott Greenwood of the American Civil Liberties Union (ACLU) said at the September 2013 conference:

> The average interaction between an officer and a citizen in an urban area is already recorded in multiple ways. The citizen may record it on his phone. If there is some conflict happening, one or more witnesses may record it. Often there are fixed security cameras nearby that capture the interaction. So the thing that makes the most sense—if you really want accountability both for your officers and for the people they interact with—is to also have video from the officer's perspective.

The use of body-worn cameras also raises important questions about privacy and trust. What are the privacy issues associated with recording victims of crime? How can officers maintain positive community relationships if they are ordered to record almost every type of interaction with the public? Will members of the public find it off-putting to be told by an officer, "I am recording this encounter," particularly if the encounter is a casual one? Do body-worn cameras also undermine the trust between officers and their superiors within the police department?

In addition to these overarching issues, police leaders must also consider many practical policy issues, including the significant financial costs of deploying cameras and storing recorded data, training requirements, and rules and systems that must be adopted to ensure that body-worn camera video cannot be accessed for improper reasons.

"Because technology is advancing faster than policy, it's important that we keep having discussions about what these new tools mean for us. We have to ask ourselves the hard questions. What do these technologies mean for constitutional policing? We have to keep debating the advantages and disadvantages. If we embrace this new technology, we have to make sure that we are using it to help us do our jobs better."

– Charles Ramsey, Police Commissioner, Philadelphia Police Department

---

1. Body-worn cameras are small video cameras—typically attached to an officer's clothing, helmet, or sunglasses—that can capture, from an officer's point of view, video and audio recordings of activities, including traffic stops, arrests, searches, interrogations, and critical incidents such as officer-involved shootings.

Project overview

Even as police departments are increasingly adopting body-worn cameras, many questions about this technology have yet to be answered. In an effort to address these questions and produce policy guidance to law enforcement agencies, the Police Executive Research Forum (PERF), with support from the U.S. Department of Justice's Office of Community Oriented Policing Services (COPS Office), conducted research in 2013 on the use of body-worn cameras. This research project consisted of three major components: an informal survey of 500 law enforcement agencies nationwide; interviews with police executives; and a conference in which police chiefs and other experts from across the country gathered to discuss the use of body-worn cameras.

First, PERF distributed surveys to 500 police departments nationwide in July 2013. The exploratory survey was designed to examine the nationwide usage of body-worn cameras and to identify the primary issues that need to be considered. Questions covered topics such as recording requirements; whether certain officers are required to wear body-worn cameras; camera placement on the body; and data collection, storage, and review.

PERF received responses from 254 departments (a 51 percent response rate). Although the use of body-worn cameras is undoubtedly a growing trend, over 75 percent of the respondents reported that they did not use body-worn cameras as of July 2013.

> *"I really believe that body-worn cameras are the wave of the future for most police agencies. This technology is driving the expectations of the public. They see this out there, and they see that other agencies that have it, and their question is, 'Why don't you have it?'"*
>
> – Roberto Villaseñor, Chief of Police, Tucson (Arizona) Police Department

Of the 63 agencies that reported using body-worn cameras, nearly one-third did not have a written policy governing body-worn camera usage. Many police executives reported that their hesitance to implement a written policy was due to a lack of guidance on what the policies should include, which highlights the need for a set of standards and best practices regarding body-worn cameras.

Second, PERF staff members interviewed more than 40 police executives whose departments have implemented—or have considered implementing—body-worn cameras. As part of this process, PERF also reviewed written policies on body-worn cameras that were shared by departments across the country.

Last, PERF convened a one-day conference of more than 200 police chiefs, sheriffs, scholars, representatives from federal criminal justice agencies, and other experts to discuss the policy and operational issues surrounding body-worn cameras. The conference, held in Washington, D.C., on September 11, 2013, gave participants the opportunity to share the lessons they have learned, to identify promising practices from the field, and to engage in a dialogue about the many unresolved issues regarding the use of body-worn cameras.

Drawing upon feedback from the conference, the survey results, and information gathered from the interviews and policy reviews, PERF created this publication to provide law enforcement agencies with guidance on the use of body-worn cameras.

The first chapter discusses the perceived benefits of deploying body-worn cameras, particularly how law enforcement agencies have used the cameras to resolve complaints and prevent spurious complaints, to enhance transparency and officer accountability, to identify and address structural problems within the department, and to provide an important new type of evidence for criminal and internal administrative investigations.

The second chapter discusses the larger policy concerns that agencies must consider when implementing body-worn cameras, including privacy implications, the effect cameras have on community relationships and community policing, officers' concerns, the expectations cameras create, and financial costs.

The third chapter presents PERF's policy recommendations, which reflect the promising practices and lessons that emerged from PERF's conference and its extensive discussions with police executives and other experts following the conference.

The police executives referenced throughout this publication are those who attended the September conference; participated in a discussion of body-worn cameras at PERF's October 2013 Town Hall Meeting, a national forum held in Philadelphia; provided policies for PERF's review; and/or were interviewed by PERF in late-2013 and early-2014.[2] A list of participants from the September conference is located in appendix B.

---

2. The titles listed throughout this document reflect officials' positions at the time of the September 2013 conference.

Chapter 1. Perceived Benefits of Body-Worn Cameras

Among the police executives whose departments use body-worn cameras, there is an overall perception that the cameras provide a useful tool for law enforcement. For these agencies, the perceived benefits that body-worn cameras offer—capturing a video recording of critical incidents and encounters with the public, strengthening police accountability, and providing a valuable new type of evidence—largely outweigh the potential drawbacks. For example, Chief Superintendent Stephen Cullen of the New South Wales (Australia) Police Force said, "After testing out body-worn cameras, we were convinced that it was the way of the future for policing."

Accountability and transparency

The police executives whom PERF consulted cited many ways in which body-worn cameras have helped their agencies strengthen accountability and transparency. These officials said that, by providing a video record of police activity, body-worn cameras have made their operations more transparent to the public and have helped resolve questions following an encounter between officers and members of the public. These officials also said that body-worn cameras are helping to prevent problems from arising in the first place by increasing officer professionalism, helping agencies evaluate and improve officer performance, and allowing agencies to identify and correct larger structural problems within the department. As a result, they report that their agencies are experiencing fewer complaints and that encounters between officers and the public have improved.

> "Everyone is on their best behavior when the cameras are running. The officers, the public—everyone."
>
> – Ron Miller, Chief of Police, Topeka (Kansas) Police Department

Reducing complaints and resolving officer-involved incidents

In 2012, the police department in Rialto, California, in partnership with the University of Cambridge-Institute of Criminology (UK), examined whether body-worn cameras would have any impact on the number of complaints against officers or on officers' use of force. Over the course of one year, the department randomly assigned body-worn cameras to various front-line officers across 988 shifts. The study found that there was a 60 percent reduction in officer use of force incidents following camera deployment, and during the experiment, the shifts without cameras experienced twice as many use of force incidents as shifts with cameras. The study also found that there was an 88 percent reduction in the number of citizen complaints between the year prior to camera implementation and the year following deployment.[3] Chief of Police William Farrar of Rialto, who oversaw the study, said, "Whether the reduced number of complaints was because of the officers behaving better or the citizens behaving better—well, it was probably a little bit of both."

A study conducted in Mesa, Arizona, also found that body-worn cameras were associated with a reduction in complaints against officers. In October 2012, the Mesa Police Department implemented a one-year pilot program in which 50 officers were assigned to wear body-worn cameras, and 50 officers were assigned to a control group without the cameras. The two groups were demographically

Body-worn camera results for Rialto (California) Police Department

- 60 percent reduction in officer use of force incidents following camera deployment
- Half the number of use of force incidents for shifts with cameras compared to shifts without cameras
- 88 percent reduction in number of citizen complaints between the year prior to and following camera deployment

---

3. William Farrar, "Operation Candid Camera: Rialto Police Department's Body-Worn Camera Experiment," *The Police Chief* 81 (2014): 20–25.

similar in terms of age, race, and other characteristics. The study, which was conducted by Arizona State University, found that during the first eight months of deployment, the officers without the cameras had almost three times as many complaints as the officers who wore the cameras.[4] The study also found that the officers assigned body-worn cameras had 40 percent fewer total complaints and 75 percent fewer use of force complaints during the pilot program than they did during the prior year when they were not wearing cameras.[5]

Body-worn camera results for Mesa (Arizona) Police Department

- Nearly 3x more complaints against officers without cameras, eight months after camera deployment

- 40 percent fewer total complaints for officers with cameras during pilot program

- 75 percent fewer use of force complaints for officers with cameras during pilot program

Police executives interviewed by PERF overwhelmingly report that their agencies experienced a noticeable drop in complaints against officers after deploying body-worn cameras. "There's absolutely no doubt that having body-worn cameras reduces the number of complaints against officers," said Chief of Police Ron Miller of Topeka, Kansas. One explanation for this is that the mere presence of a camera can lead to more civil interactions between officers and the public. "We actually encourage our officers to let people know that they are recording," said Chief of Police Ken Miller of Greensboro, North Carolina. "Why? Because we think that it elevates behavior on both sides of the camera."

Lieutenant Harold Rankin, who oversaw the body-worn camera program in Mesa, agrees: "Anytime you know you're being recorded, it's going to have an impact on your behavior. When our officers encounter a confrontational situation, they'll tell the person that the camera is running. That's often enough to deescalate the situation." Many police executives report that wearing cameras has helped improve professionalism among their officers. Chief Superintendent Cullen of New South Wales said, "After testing out body-worn cameras, the overwhelming response from officers was that the cameras increased their professionalism because they knew that everything they said and did was being recorded."

"In the testing we did [of body-worn cameras], we had a number of tenured officers who wanted to wear the cameras and try them out, and their feedback was very positive. They said things like, 'You'll be amazed at how people stop acting badly when you say this is a camera, even if they're intoxicated.' And we also know that the overwhelming majority of our officers are out there doing a very good job, and the cameras will show just that."

– Douglas Gillespie, Sheriff, Las Vegas Metropolitan Police Department

Many agencies have found that having video footage of an encounter also discourages people from filing unfounded complaints against officers. "We've actually had citizens come into the department to file a complaint, but after we show them the video, they literally turn and walk back out," said Chief Miller of Topeka. Chief of Police Michael Frazier of Surprise, Arizona, reports a similar experience. "Recently we received an allegation that an officer engaged in racial profiling during a traffic stop. The officer was wearing his body-worn camera, and the footage showed that the allegation was completely unfounded," Frazier said. "After reviewing the tape, the complainants admitted that they have never been treated unfavorably by any officers in my department." As several police officials noted, preventing unfounded complaints can save departments the significant amounts of time and money spent on lengthy investigations and lawsuits.

When questions arise following an encounter, police executives said that having a video record of events helps lead to a quicker resolution. According to the results of PERF's exploratory survey, the number one reason why police departments choose to implement body-worn cameras is to provide a more accurate documentation of police encounters with the public. Police executives report that when questions arise following an encounter or a major event such as an officer-involved shooting, having video from a body-worn camera can help resolve the questions.

---

4. Harold Rankin, "End of Program Evaluation and Recommendations: On-Officer Body Camera System" (Mesa, AZ: Mesa Police Department, 2013).
5. Ibid.

Agencies are also reporting that, in most of these cases, the resolution is in support of the officer's account of events. Chief of Police Mike Chitwood of Daytona Beach, Florida, recalled one example in which a member of the public threatened to file a complaint against officers following a contentious encounter. Alleging that the officers had threatened him and used racial epithets, the individual said that he would go to the news media if the department failed to take action. One of the officers involved had been wearing a body-worn camera. "We reviewed the video, and clearly the individual lied," recalled Chitwood. "The officer was glad to have the footage because the individual's allegations were absolutely not what was represented in the video."

Body-worn cameras have also helped to resolve more serious incidents, including officer-involved shootings. Chief Miller of Topeka said that the local district attorney cleared an officer in a deadly shooting incident after viewing the officer's body-worn camera footage. Miller described how the camera footage captured the event in real time and provided a record of events that would otherwise not have existed. "The entire event was captured on video from the perspective of the officer. Now tell me when that happened before the advent of body-worn cameras," said Miller.

Several police departments, including those in Daytona Beach, Florida, and Greenville, North Carolina, are finding that officers with a history of complaints are now actively requesting to wear cameras. For officers who behave properly but generate complaints because they have high levels of activity or frequent contacts with criminal suspects, cameras can be seen as beneficial. "We all have our small percentage of officers with a history of complaints," said Chief of Police Hassan Aden of Greenville. "Internal Affairs has told me that these officers have come in to request body-worn cameras so that they can be protected in the future."

> *"The use of body-worn video by frontline officers has real potential to reduce complaints of incivility and use of force by officers. The footage can also exonerate officers from vexatious and malicious complaints. In addition, I feel there are benefits to the criminal justice system in terms of more guilty pleas, reduced costs at court, and a reduction in the number of civil cases brought against the police service for unlawful arrest/excessive force. We already have good examples of body-worn video footage exonerating officers from malicious complaints."*
>
> – Paul Rumney, Detective Chief Superintendent, Greater Manchester (UK) Police

Identifying and correcting internal agency problems

Another way that body-worn cameras have strengthened accountability and transparency, according to many police executives, is by helping agencies identify and correct problems within the department. In fact, PERF's survey found that 94 percent of respondents use body-worn camera footage to train officers and aid in administrative reviews.

Many police agencies are discovering that body-worn cameras can serve as a useful training tool to help improve officer performance. For example, agencies are using footage from body-worn cameras to provide scenario-based training, to evaluate the performance of new officers in the field, and to identify new areas in which training is needed. By using body-worn cameras in this way, agencies have the opportunity to raise standards of performance when it comes to tactics, communication, and customer service. This can help increase the perceived legitimacy and sense of procedural justice that communities have about their police departments.

Law enforcement agencies have also found that body-worn cameras can help them to identify officers who abuse their authority or commit other misconduct and to assist in correcting questionable behavior before it reaches that level. In Phoenix, for example, an officer was fired after his body-worn camera captured repeated incidents of unprofessional conduct. Following a complaint

> *"We have about 450 body-worn cameras actively deployed, and in the overwhelming majority of cases, the footage demonstrates that the officer's actions were appropriate."*
>
> – Sean Whent, Chief of Police, Oakland (California) Police Department

against the officer, the police department reviewed footage from the incident along with video from prior shifts. Upon finding repeated instances of verbal abuse, profanity, and threats against members of the public, the department terminated the officer. "It clearly shocked the conscience when you saw all of the different incidents," said Assistant Chief of Police Dave Harvey of Phoenix.

In Daytona Beach, Chief Chitwood requested that the officers with a history of complaints be among the first to be outfitted with body-worn cameras. Although he found that usually the videos demonstrated that "the majority of the officers are hardworking, good police," he has also seen how body-worn cameras can help an agency address discipline problems. Chitwood said:

> We had an officer who had several questionable incidents in the past, so we outfitted him with a camera. Right in the middle of an encounter with a subject, the camera goes blank, and then it comes back on when the incident is over. He said that the camera malfunctioned, so we gave him another one. A week later he goes to arrest a woman, and again, the camera goes blank just before the encounter. He claimed again that the camera had malfunctioned. So we conducted a forensic review of the camera, which determined that the officer had intentionally hit the power button right before the camera shut off. Our policy says that if you turn it off, you're done. He resigned the next day.

Body-worn cameras can also help law enforcement officials to address wide-reaching structural problems within the department. Many police officials that PERF consulted said that body-worn cameras have allowed them to identify potential weaknesses within their agencies and to develop solutions for improvement, such as offering new training programs or revising their departmental policies and protocols.

In Phoenix, an officer was fired after his body-worn camera captured repeated incidents of unprofessional conduct.

For example, Chief of Police William Lansdowne of San Diego said that one reason his department is implementing body-worn cameras is to improve its understanding of incidents involving claims of racial profiling. "When it comes to collecting data, the raw numbers don't always fully capture the true scope of a problem," he said. "But by capturing an audio and video account of an encounter, cameras provide an objective record of whether racial profiling took place, what patterns of officer behavior are present, and how often the problem occurs."

Police agencies have also found that implementing a body-worn camera program can be useful when facing consent decrees and external investigations. Roy Austin, deputy assistant attorney general for the Civil Rights Division at the U.S. Department of Justice, said, "We want to get police departments out from under consent decrees as soon as possible. What is important is whether you can show that your officers are engaged in constitutional policing on a regular basis. Although it isn't an official Department of Justice policy, the Civil Rights Division believes that body-worn cameras can be useful for doing that."

Many police departments that have faced external investigations, including those in New Orleans and Detroit, are in various stages of testing and implementing body-worn cameras. Police executives in these cities said that cameras help them to demonstrate they are improving policies and practices within their agencies. Police Superintendent Ron Serpas of New Orleans, whose department is in the process of deploying more than 400 body-worn cameras, said, "Body-worn cameras will be good for us. The hardworking officers say, 'Chief, just give us a chance to show everyone that we are not like the people who went astray after Hurricane Katrina.' The one thing that New Orleans police officers want more than anything else is the independent verification that they are doing what they're supposed to do." The police departments in Las Vegas, Nevada, and Spokane, Washington are also implementing body-worn cameras to assist in complying with the collaborative agreements they entered into with the COPS Office of the U.S. Department of Justice.

Chief of Police Charlie Beck of Los Angeles, whose department is testing body-worn cameras, understands first-hand how video evidence can help in these situations. "We exited our consent decree last year, and one of the reasons that the federal judge signed off on us was that we implemented in-car video," said Beck. "Recordings can help improve public trust."

Evidence documentation

Police executives said that body-worn cameras have significantly improved how officers capture evidence for investigations and court proceedings. Along with documenting encounters with members of the public, body-worn cameras can provide a record of interrogations and arrests, as well as what officers witness at crime scenes.

Chief of Police Jason Parker of Dalton, Georgia, described how body-worn cameras have helped officers to improve evidence collection at accident scenes. "It is always hard to gather evidence from accident scenes," Parker said. He explained that officers are often focused on securing the scene and performing life-saving measures and that witnesses and victims may not always remember what they had told officers in the confusion. This can lead to conflicting reports when victims and witnesses are asked to repeat their accounts in later statements. "Unlike in-car cameras, body-worn cameras capture everything that happens as officers travel around the scene and interview multiple people. The body-worn cameras have been incredibly useful in accurately preserving information."

Some prosecutors have started encouraging police departments to use body-worn cameras to capture more reliable evidence for court, particularly in matters like domestic violence cases that can be difficult to prosecute. Chief Chitwood of Daytona Beach explained how body-worn cameras have changed how domestic violence cases are handled. "Oftentimes we know that the suspect is repeatedly abusing the victim, but either the victim refuses to press charges, or there is simply not enough evidence to go to trial," he said. With the victim's consent, Daytona Beach officers can now use body-worn cameras to videotape victim statements. "The footage shows first-hand the victim's injuries, demeanor, and immediate reactions," Chitwood noted. In some cases, officers capture the assault itself on video if they arrive on the scene while the incident is still ongoing. "This means that we can have enough evidence to move forward with the case, even if the victim ultimately declines to prosecute."

Chief Miller of Topeka echoed this sentiment: "When we show suspects in domestic violence cases footage from the body-worn cameras, often they plead guilty without even having to go to trial."

> *"Some police departments are doing themselves a disservice by not using body-worn cameras. Everyone around you is going to have a camera, and so everyone else is going to be able to tell the story better than you if you don't have these cameras. And when the Civil Rights Division is looking at a police department, every piece of information that shows the department is engaged in constitutional policing is important. So of course body-worn cameras can help."*
>
> – Roy L. Austin, Jr., Deputy Assistant Attorney General, Civil Rights Division, U.S. Department of Justice

> *"Although body-worn cameras are just one tool, the quality of information that they can capture is unsurpassed. With sound policy and guidance, their evidentiary value definitely outweighs any drawbacks or concerns."*
>
> – Jason Parker, Chief of Police, Dalton (Georgia) Police Department

Chapter 2. Considerations for Implementation

New technologies in policing raise numerous policy issues that must be considered. This is especially true with body-worn cameras, which can have significant implications in terms of privacy, community relationships, and internal departmental affairs. As agencies develop body-worn camera programs, it is crucial that they thoughtfully examine how their policies and practices intersect with these larger questions. Policy issues to look at include the effect these cameras have on privacy and community relationships, the concerns raised by frontline officers, the expectations that cameras create in terms of court proceedings and officer credibility, and the financial considerations that cameras present.

Privacy considerations

The proliferation of camera phones, advances in surveillance technology, and the emergence of social media have changed the way people view privacy, contributing to the sense that, as Police Commissioner Charles Ramsey of Philadelphia said, it sometimes feels as though "everyone is filming everybody." As technology advances and expectations of privacy evolve, it is critical that law enforcement agencies carefully consider how the technology they use affects the public's privacy rights, especially when courts have not yet provided guidance on these issues.

Body-worn cameras raise many privacy issues that have not been considered before. Unlike many traditional surveillance methods, body-worn cameras can simultaneously record both audio and video and capture close-up images that allow for the potential use of facial recognition technology. In addition, while stationary surveillance cameras generally cover only public spaces, body-worn cameras give officers the ability to record inside private homes and to film sensitive situations that might emerge during calls for service.

"In London we have CCTVs, which are quite extensive and becoming even more so, but the distinction is that those cameras don't listen to your conversations. They observe behavior and see what people do and cover public space, so you can see if there is a crime being committed. But CCTVs don't generally seek out individuals. So I think there is an important distinction there."

– Sir Bernard Hogan-Howe, Commissioner, London Metropolitan Police Service

There is also concern about how the footage from body-worn cameras might be stored and used. For example, will a person be able to obtain video that was recorded inside a neighbor's home? Will agencies keep videos indefinitely? Is it possible that the body-worn camera footage might be improperly posted online?

When implementing body-worn cameras, law enforcement agencies must balance these privacy considerations with the need for transparency of police operations, accurate documentation of events, and evidence collection. This means making careful decisions about when officers will be required to activate cameras, how long recorded data should be retained, who has access to the footage, who owns the recorded data, and how to handle internal and external requests for disclosure.

Determining when to record

The issue with perhaps the greatest privacy implications is deciding which types of encounters and activities officers should record. Should officers be required to record every interaction with a member of the public? Or are there some situations in which recording should be discretionary or prohibited?

One approach is to require officers to record all encounters with the public. This would require officers to activate their cameras not only during calls for service or other law enforcement-related encounters but also during informal conversations with members of the public (e.g., a person asking an officer for directions or an officer stopping into a store and engaging in casual conversation with the owner). This is the approach advocated by the American Civil Liberties Union (ACLU), which stated in a report released in October 2013, "If a police department is to place its cameras under officer control, then it must put in place tightly effective means of limiting officers' ability to choose which encounters to record. That can only take the form of a department-wide policy that mandates that police turn on recording during every interaction with the public."[6]

Scott Greenwood, an attorney with the ACLU, explained why the ACLU advocates recording all encounters. "You don't want to give officers a list and say, 'Only record the following 10 types of situations.' You want officers to record all the situations, so when a situation does go south, there's an unimpeachable record of it—good, bad, ugly, all of it. This is an optimal policy from a civil liberties perspective."

Greenwood said this approach benefits not only the public but also officers. "Mandatory recording is also what will protect an officer from allegations of discretionary recording or tampering," said Greenwood. "You want activating the camera to be a reflexive decision, not something that officers have to evaluate with each new situation. If officers have to determine what type of incident it is before recording, there are going to be a lot of situations in which a recording might have exonerated an officer, but the recording was never made."

However, PERF believes that requiring officers to record every encounter with the public would sometimes undermine community members' privacy rights and damage important police-community relationships. There are certain situations, such as interviews with crime victims and witnesses and informal, non-law enforcement interactions with members of the community, that call for affording officers some measure of discretion in determining whether to activate their cameras. There are situations in which not recording is a reasonable decision. An agency's body-worn camera policy should expressly describe these situations and provide solid guidance for officers when they exercise discretion not to record.

For example, officer discretion is needed in sensitive situations, such as encounters with crime victims or witnesses who are concerned about retaliation if they are seen as cooperating with the police. In other cases, officer discretion is needed for routine and casual situations—such as officers on foot or bike patrol who wish to chat with neighborhood residents—and turning on a video camera could make the encounter seem officious and off-putting.

> *"For the [American Civil Liberties Union], the challenge of on-officer cameras is the tension between their potential to invade privacy and their strong benefit in promoting police accountability. Overall, we think they can be a win-win—but only if they are deployed within a framework of strong policies to ensure they protect the public without becoming yet another system for routine sur-veillance of the public, and maintain public confidence in the integrity of those privacy protections. Without such a framework, their accountability benefits would not exceed their privacy risks."*
>
> – "Police Body-Mounted Cameras: With Right Policies in Place, a Win for All" (New York: ACLU, 2013).

---

6.   Jay Stanley, "Police Body-Mounted Cameras: With Right Policies in Place, a Win for All" (New York: ACLU, 2013), https://www.aclu.org/files/assets/police_body-mounted_cameras.pdf.

Of the police departments that PERF consulted, very few have adopted the policy of recording all encounters with the public. The more common approach is to require officers to activate their cameras when responding to calls for service and during law enforcement-related encounters and activities, such as traffic stops, arrests, searches, interrogations, and pursuits. In many cases, the department's written policy defines what constitutes a law enforcement-related encounter or activity, and some policies also provide a specific list of which activities are included. Many policies generally indicate that when in doubt, officers should record. Most policies also give officers the discretion to not record when doing so would be unsafe, impossible, or impractical, but most require officers to articulate in writing their reasons for not activating the camera or to say on camera why they are turning the camera off.

Police executives cite several reasons for favoring a more limited and flexible approach rather than requiring officers to record all encounters. One reason is that it gives officers the discretion to not record if they feel that doing so would infringe on an individual's privacy rights. For example, many police departments, including those in Oakland and Rialto, California; Mesa, Arizona; and Fort Collins, Colorado, give officers discretion regarding whether to record interviews with victims of rape, abuse, or other sensitive crimes. Some departments also extend this discretion to recording victims of other crimes. The Daytona Beach (Florida) Police Department recently changed its policy to require that officers obtain consent, on camera, from all crime victims prior to recording an interview. "This new policy is a response to the privacy concerns that arise when you are dealing with victims of crime," said Chief of Police Mike Chitwood of Daytona Beach.

> *Of the police departments that PERF consulted, very few have adopted the policy of recording all encounters with the public. The more common approach is to require officers to activate their cameras when responding to calls for service and during law enforcement-related encounters and activities, such as traffic stops, arrests, searches, interrogations, and pursuits.*

Some agencies encourage officers to use discretion when determining whether to record encounters with or searches of individuals who are partially or completely unclothed. Chief of Police Don Lanpher of Aberdeen, South Dakota, said, "We had an incident when officers were called to assist a female on a landing in an apartment building who was partially undressed. All of the officers had cameras, but they did not record her until she was covered. Officers are encouraged to use discretion in those cases."

In addition to privacy concerns, police executives cite the potential negative impact on community relationships as a reason for not requiring officers to record all encounters with the public. Their goal, always, is to maintain an open dialogue with community members and preserve the trust in their relationships.[7] "There are a lot of issues with recording every citizen contact without regard to how cooperative or adversarial it is," said Chief of Police Ken Miller of Greensboro, North Carolina. "If people think that they are going to be recorded every time they talk to an officer, regardless of the context, it is going to damage openness and create barriers to important relationships."

Commissioner Ramsey of Philadelphia agrees. "There has to be some measure of discretion. If you have a police interaction as a result of a 911 call or a reasonable suspicion stop, it is one thing—you should record in those situations. But you have to give officers discretion whether to record if they are just saying 'hello' to someone or if they are approached by an individual who wants to give them information."

---

7. See "Impact on community relationships" on page 19, "Securing community support" on page 21, "Protecting intelligence-gathering efforts" on page 22, and "Lessons learned about impact on community relationships" on page 24 for strategies departments have taken to address this impact.

Some police executives also believe that requiring officers to record all encounters can signal a lack of trust in officers, which is problematic for any department that wants to encourage its officers to be thoughtful and to show initiative. For example, a survey of officers conducted in Vacaville, California, found that although 70 percent of officers were in favor of using body-worn cameras, a majority were opposed to a policy containing strict requirements of mandatory recording of all police contacts.

"In a sensitive investigation, such as a rape or child abuse case, if you have a victim who doesn't want to be recorded, I think you have to take that into account. I think that you cannot just arbitrarily film every encounter. There are times when you've got to give your officers some discretion to turn the camera off. Of course, the officers should be required to articulate why they're not recording or why they're shutting it off, but we have to give them that discretion."

– Charlie Beck, Chief of Police, Los Angeles Police Department

For departments whose polices do not require officers to record every interaction with the public, the goal is to sufficiently ensure accountability and adherence to the department's body-worn camera policies and protocols. For example, when officers have discretion to not record an encounter, many departments require them to document, either on camera or in writing, the fact that they did not record and their reasons for not recording. Some departments also require officers to obtain supervisor approval to deactivate the camera if a subject requests to not be recorded.

Consent to record

In a handful of states, officers are legally required to inform subjects when they are recording and to obtain the person's consent to record. This is known as a "two-party consent" law, and it can create challenges to implementing a body-worn camera program. In many two-party consent states, however, police executives have successfully worked with their state legislatures to have the consent requirement waived for body-worn police cameras. For example, in February 2014 Pennsylvania enacted a law waiving the two-party consent requirement for police using body-worn cameras.[8] Efforts are under way to change two-party consent statutes in other jurisdictions as well. Each department must research its state laws to determine whether the two-party consent requirement applies.

"Legitimacy in policing is built on trust. And the notion of video-recording every interaction in a very tense situation would simply not be a practical operational way of delivering policing. In fact, it would exacerbate all sorts of problems. In the United Kingdom, we're also subject to human rights legislation, laws on right to privacy, right to family life, and I'm sure you have similar statutes. It's far more complicated than a blanket policy of 'every interaction is filmed.' I think that's far too simplistic. We have to give our officers some discretion. We cannot have a policy that limits discretion of officers to a point where using these devices has a negative effect on community-police relations."

– Sir Hugh Orde, President, Association of Chief Police Officers (UK)

Some police executives believe that it is good practice for officers to inform people when they are recording, even if such disclosures are not required by law. In Greensboro, for example, officers are encouraged—but not required—to announce when they are recording. Chief Miller of Greensboro said this policy is based on the belief that the knowledge that cameras are running can help defuse potentially confrontational situations and improve behavior from all parties.

However, many police executives in one-party consent states do not explicitly instruct officers to inform people that they are recording. "Kansas is a one-party consent state, so only the officer needs to know that the camera is running. But if a person asks, the officer tells them the truth," said Chief of Police Ron Miller of Topeka, Kansas.

---

8. Police body cameras heading to Pennsylvania (February 10, 2014), ABC 27 News, http://www.abc27.com/story/24686416/police-body-cameras-heading-to-pennsylvania.

Recording inside private homes

Another privacy question is whether and under what conditions officers should be allowed to record while inside a person's home. Many law enforcement agencies have taken the position that officers have the right to record inside a private home as long as they have a legal right to be there. According to this approach, if an officer enters a home in response to a call for service, pursuant to a valid search warrant, or with consent of the resident, officers can record what they find inside.

There is a concern that footage taken inside a private home may be subject to public disclosure. Deputy Chief of Police William Roseman of Albuquerque described how this can be particularly problematic in states with broad public disclosure laws. "Here in Albuquerque, everything is open to public record unless it is part of an ongoing investigation. So if police come into your house and it is captured on video, and if the video isn't being used in an investigation, your neighbor can request the footage under the open records act, and we must give it to them." Scott Greenwood of the ACLU has expressed similar concerns:

> An officer might be allowed to go into the residence and record, but that does not mean that everything inside ought to be public record. The warrant is an exception to the Fourth Amendment, not a waiver. We do not want this to show up on YouTube. My next-door neighbor should never be able to view something that happened inside my house without my permission.

"One of the things we are forgetting is that we already send officers into people's homes and have them document all these bits of information that we're worried about recording. If an officer enters someone's home, they document the condition of the home, especially if it's a case about a child or involves domestic violence or physical injury. So videos are just a technologically advanced type of police report that should be treated no differently from an initial contact form that we currently fill out every day. The advantage of a camera is now you have a factual representation as opposed to an interpretation by an officer."

– Chris Burbank, Chief of Police,
Salt Lake City (Utah) Police Department

Data storage, retention, and disclosure

Decisions about where to store video footage and how long to keep it can have a far-reaching effect on privacy. Many police executives believe that privacy concerns can be addressed through data storage, retention, and disclosure policies. However, when developing these policies, agency leaders must balance privacy considerations with other factors, such as state law requirements, transparency, and data storage capacity and cost.

Data storage policies

Among police executives interviewed by PERF, security, reliability, cost, and technical capacity were the primary factors cited for choosing a particular method for storing video files from body-worn cameras. Among the more than 40 departments that PERF consulted, all stored body-worn camera video on an in-house server (managed internally) or an online cloud database (managed by a third-party vendor).[9]

Police executives noted a number of strategies that can help agencies protect the integrity and privacy of their recorded data, regardless of which storage method is used. These lessons learned regarding data storage include the following:

- *Consult with prosecutors and legal advisors:* Legal experts can advise whether data storage policies and practices are in compliance with all relevant laws and adequately preserve evidentiary chain of custody.

---

9.   Cloud storage is a method for storing and backing up electronic data. The data is maintained and managed remotely, generally by a third party, and made available to users over a network, or "cloud."

- *Explicitly prohibit data tampering, editing, and copying.*

- *Include protections against tampering with the data prior to downloading:* This helps to mitigate concerns that officers will be able to alter or delete recordings prior to downloading them. Some body-worn camera systems are sold with technological safeguards that make it impossible for an officer to access the data prior to downloading.

- *Create an auditing system:* It is important to have a record of who accesses video data, when, and for what purpose. Some storage systems include a built-in audit trail.

- *Explicitly state who will be authorized to access data:* Many written policies outline who will have access to the data (e.g., supervisors, Internal Affairs, certain other officers and department personnel, and prosecutors) and for what purpose (e.g., administrative review, training, and investigations).

- *Ensure there is a reliable back-up system:* Some systems have a built-in backup system that preserves recorded data, and some departments copy recordings to disc and store them as evidence.

- *Specify when videos will be downloaded from the camera to the storage system and who will download them:* The majority of existing policies require the camera operator to download the footage by the end of each shift. In the case of an officer-involved shooting or other serious incident, some policies require supervisors to step in and physically take possession of the camera and assume downloading responsibilities.

> *"Whether you store video internally or externally, protecting the data and preserving the chain of custody should always be a concern. Either way, you need something built into the system so that you know that video has not been altered."*
>
> – Ken Miller, Chief of Police, Greensboro (North Carolina) Police Department

- *Consider third-party vendors carefully:* Overwhelmingly, the police executives whom PERF interviewed reported that their legal advisors and prosecutors were comfortable using a third-party vendor to manage the storage system. When deciding whether to use a third-party vendor, departments consider the vendor's technical assistance capabilities and whether the system includes protections such as an audit trail, backup system, etc. Police executives stressed the importance of entering into a legal contract with the vendor that protects the agency's data.

These strategies are important not only for protecting the privacy rights of the people recorded but also for preserving evidence and resolving allegations of data tampering.

Data retention policies

The length of time that departments retain body-worn camera footage plays a key role for privacy. The longer that recorded videos are retained, the longer they are subject to public disclosure, which can be problematic if the video contains footage associated with privacy concerns. And community members' concerns about police departments collecting data about them in the first place are lessened if the videos are not retained for long periods of time.

The retention times are generally dictated by the type of encounter or incident that the footage captures. Although protocols vary by department, footage is typically categorized as either "evidentiary" or "non-evidentiary."

Evidentiary video involves footage of an incident or encounter that could prove useful for investigative purposes, such as a crime, an arrest or citation, a search, a use of force incident, or a confrontational encounter with a member of the public. Evidentiary footage is usually further categorized by specific incident type, and the retention period is governed by state evidentiary rules for that incident. For example, many state laws require that footage involving a homicide be retained indefinitely, but video of a traffic citation must be kept for only a matter of months. Departments often purge evidentiary videos at the conclusion of the investigation, court proceeding, or administrative hearing for which they were used.

Non-evidentiary video involves footage that does necessarily have value to aid in an investigation or prosecution, such as footage of an incident or encounter that does not lead to an arrest or citation or of general activities that an officer might perform while on duty (e.g., assisting a motorist or clearing a roadway). Agencies often have more leeway in setting retention times for non-evidentiary videos, which are generally not subject to state evidentiary laws.

Of the departments that PERF consulted, the most common retention time for non-evidentiary video was between 60 and 90 days. Some departments retain non-evidentiary video for an even shorter period. Fort Collins, Colorado, for example, discards footage after seven days if there is no citizen contact recorded and after 30 days if contact is made but no enforcement action is taken. On the other end of the spectrum, some departments, such as Albuquerque, retain non-evidentiary video for a full year.

Many police executives express a preference for shorter retention times for non-evidentiary video. Shorter retention periods not only address privacy concerns but also reduce the costs associated with data storage. On the other hand, police executives noted that they must keep videos long enough to demonstrate transparency and to have footage of an encounter in case a complaint arises about an officer's actions. For example, departments in Rialto, Fort Collins, Albuquerque, Daytona Beach, and Toronto base retention times in part on how long it generally takes for complaints to be filed.

Public disclosure policies

State public disclosure laws, often known as freedom of information laws, govern when footage from body-worn cameras is subject to public release. However, most of these laws were written long before law enforcement agencies began deploying body-worn cameras, so the laws do not necessarily account for all of the considerations that must be made when police departments undertake a body-worn camera program.

"It is important to have retention policies that are directly linked to the purposes of having the video, whether that purpose is to have evidence of a crime or to hold officers and the public accountable. Agencies should not retain every video indefinitely, or else those videos could be used down the road for all sorts of inappropriate reasons."

– Lorie Fridell, Associate Professor, University of South Florida

Although broad disclosure policies can promote police agency transparency and accountability, some videos—especially recordings of victims or from inside people's homes—will raise privacy concerns if they are released to the public or the news media. When determining how to approach public disclosure issues, law enforcement agencies must balance the legitimate interest of openness with protecting privacy rights.[10]

In most state public disclosure laws, exceptions are outlined that may exempt body-worn camera footage from public release. For example, even the broadest disclosure laws typically contain an exception for video that contains evidence or is part of an ongoing investigation. Some state disclosure laws, such as those in North Carolina, also exempt personnel records from public release. Body-worn camera videos used to monitor officer performance may fall under this type of exception.

---

10. Scott Greenwood of the ACLU recommends that police executives work with the ACLU to ensure that state disclosure laws contain adequate privacy protections for body-worn camera videos. "If interpreted too broadly, open records laws can undermine the accountability of law enforcement agencies," said Greenwood. "You want to make sure that the video is not subject to arbitrary disclosure. It deserves the highest level of protection."

These exceptions to public disclosure can help police departments to avoid being required to release videos if doing so could jeopardize a criminal prosecution. The exceptions can also help police to protect the privacy of crime victims and witnesses. However, by policy and practice, law enforcement agencies should apply these exceptions judiciously to avoid any suspicion by community members that police are withholding video footage to hide officer misconduct or mistakes. In launching body-worn camera programs, law enforcement agencies should convey that their goal is to foster transparency and accountability while protecting civil liberties and privacy interests. When an agency decides whether to release or withhold body-worn camera footage of a particular incident, the agency should articulate its reasons for doing so.

> *"When developing body-worn camera policies, agencies have to consider how open the public disclosure laws are in their state. Are they going to have to give up all of their footage to any person that requests it? Or are there some protections? This is important to think about when it comes to privacy."*
>
> – Ron Miller, Chief of Police, Topeka (Kansas) Police Department

In addition, some agencies have adopted recording and retention policies that help to avoid violations of privacy. For example, some agencies allow officers to deactivate their cameras during interviews with crime victims or witnesses. And short retention times for non-evidentiary video footage can reduce the window of opportunity for requests for release of video footage that would serve no legitimate purpose.

Lessons learned on privacy considerations

In their conversations with PERF staff members, police executives and other experts revealed a number of lessons that they have learned regarding body-worn cameras and privacy rights:

- Body-worn cameras have significant implications for the public's privacy rights, particularly when it comes to recording victim interviews, nudity, and other sensitive subjects and when recording inside people's homes. Agencies must factor these privacy considerations into decisions about when to record, where and how long to store data, and how to respond to public requests for video footage.

- In terms of when officers should be required to activate their cameras, the most common approach is requiring officers to record all calls for service and law enforcement-related encounters and activities and to deactivate the camera only at the conclusion of the event or with supervisor approval.

- It is essential to clearly define what constitutes a law enforcement-related encounter or activity in the department's written body-worn camera policy. It is also useful to provide a list of specific activities that are included, noting that the list is not necessarily all inclusive. Many agencies give a general recommendation to officers that when they are in doubt, they should record.

- To protect officer safety and acknowledge that recording may not be possible in every situation, it is helpful to state in policies that recording will not be required if it would be unsafe, impossible, or impractical.

- Significant privacy concerns can arise when interviewing crime victims, particularly in situations involving rape, abuse, or other sensitive matters. Some agencies prefer to give officers discretion regarding whether to record in these circumstances. In such cases, officers should take into account the evidentiary value of recording and the willingness of the victim to speak on camera. Some agencies go a step further and require officers to obtain the victim's consent prior to recording the interview.

- To promote officer accountability, most policies require officers to document, on camera or in writing, the reasons why the officer deactivated the camera in situations that are otherwise required to be recorded.

- In one-party consent states, officers are not legally required to notify subjects when officers are recording. However, some agencies have found that announcing the camera is running promotes better behavior and defuses potentially confrontational encounters.

- When making decisions about where to store body-worn camera footage, how long to keep it, and how it should be disclosed to the public, it is advisable for agencies to consult with departmental legal counsel and prosecutors.

- Regardless of the chosen method for storing recorded data, agencies should take all possible steps to protect the integrity and security of the data. This includes explicitly stating who has access to the data and under what circumstances, creating an audit system for monitoring access, ensuring there is a reliable back-up system, specifying how data will be downloaded from the camera, and including protections against data tampering prior to downloading.

- It is important that videos be properly categorized according to the type of event contained in the footage. How the videos are categorized will determine how long they are retained, who has access, and whether they can be disclosed to the public.

- To help protect privacy rights, it is generally preferable to set shorter retention times for non-evidentiary data. The most common retention time for this video is between 60 and 90 days.

- When setting retention times, agencies should consider privacy concerns, the scope of the state's public disclosure laws, the amount of time the public needs to file complaints, and data storage capacity and costs.

- Evidentiary footage is generally exempt from public disclosure while it is part of an ongoing investigation or court proceeding. Deleting this video after it serves its evidentiary purpose can reduce the quantity of video stored and protect it from unauthorized access or release. It is important to always check whether deletion is in compliance with laws governing evidence retention.

> *In launching body-worn camera programs, law enforcement agencies should convey that their goal is to foster transparency and accountability while protecting civil liberties and privacy interests.*

- Informing the public about how long video will be retained can help promote agency transparency and accountability. Some agencies have found it useful to post retention times on the department's website.

- It is important for the agency to communicate its public disclosure policy to the community when the body-worn camera program is deployed to develop public understanding of the technology and the reasons for adopting it.

Impact on community relationships

Building positive relationships with the community is a critical aspect of policing, and these relationships can exist only if police have earned the trust of the people they serve. Police rely on these community partnerships to help them address crime and disorder issues.

At the PERF conference, a number of participants expressed concern that excessive recording with body-worn cameras may damage the relationships officers have developed with the community and hinder the openness of their community policing interactions. Some police executives fear, for example, that people will be less likely to come forward to share information if they know their conversation is going to be recorded, particularly in high-crime neighborhoods where residents might be subject to retaliation if they are seen as cooperating with police.

> *"Before we make a decision on where to go with body-worn cameras, I really think that all of us need to stop and consider some of these larger unanswered questions. We need to look at not only whether the cameras reduce complaints but also how they relate to witnesses on the street coming forward, what they mean for trust and officer credibility, and what messages they send to the public."*
>
> – Bob Cherry, Detective of Baltimore Police Department and President of Baltimore City Fraternal Order of Police

Detective Bob Cherry of the Baltimore Police Department, who is also the president of the Baltimore City Fraternal Order of Police, said, "Trust builds through relationships, and body-worn cameras start from a position of mistrust. The comments I hear from some officers are, 'I'm worried that if I wear a camera, it is going to make it hard to continue the relationship I have with a business owner or the lady down the street. These are the people I'm working with now to clean up the neighborhood.'"

Some police executives reported that deploying body-worn cameras has in fact had a negative impact on their intelligence-gathering activities, particularly when officers are not allowed the discretion to turn off the camera. Chief of Police Sean Whent of Oakland, California, explained, "Our policy is to film all detentions and to keep recording until the encounter is over. But let's say an officer detains someone, and now that person wants to give up information. We are finding that people are not inclined to do so with the camera running. We are considering changing our policy to allow officers to turn off the camera in those situations."

The Mesa (Arizona) Police Department has also found that body-worn cameras can undermine information-gathering efforts. "We have definitely seen people being more reluctant to give information when they know that they are being videotaped," said Lieutenant Harold Rankin.

However, other police executives said that these types of situations are rare and that body-worn cameras have not had a significant impact on their ability to gather information from the public. For some agencies, public reaction to the cameras has been practically nonexistent. Major Stephen Willis of the Charlotte-Mecklenburg (North Carolina) Police Department said, "We have had in-car cameras for many years, and in most instances the public has an expectation that they will be recorded. We encountered very little resistance from the public when we piloted body-worn cameras." Deputy Chief of Police Cory Christensen of Fort Collins, Colorado, said, "We are not seeing much pushback from the community. Often people do not even notice the presence of the cameras."

"I disagree that cameras hurt community relationships," said Chief of Police William Farrar of Rialto, California. "We have not seen any evidence of that. People will ask officers if they have a camera on, but it does not seem to bother them." In fact, in its evaluation of its body-worn camera program, the Rialto Police Department found that officers made 3,178 more contacts with the public (not counting calls for service) during the year that cameras were deployed than in the prior year.[11]

Some police executives reported that body-worn cameras have actually improved certain aspects of their police-community relationships. These executives said that the presence of cameras leads to better behavior by both the officer and the person being recorded. "The cameras help defuse some of the tensions that might come up during encounters with the public. I think that 98 percent of the time, cameras help improve relationships with the community," said Chief Chitwood of Daytona Beach. Deputy Chief Christensen of Fort Collins agreed: "Officers wearing cameras have reported a noticeable improvement in the quality of their encounters with the public. With both sides behaving better, community relations will improve."

11. William Farrar, "Operation Candid Camera: Rialto Police Department's Body-Worn Camera Experiment," *The Police Chief* 81 (2014): 20–25.

Sir Robert Peel's Principles of Policing

Sir Robert Peel, who created London's Metropolitan Police Force in 1829, is known as the father of modern policing. He helped to establish a policing philosophy grounded in professionalism, ethics, and strong police-community cooperation, which continues to influence policing to this day. The "Nine Principles of Policing," which were issued to the first officers of the London Metropolitan Police and reflect Sir Robert Peel's philosophy, provide guidance on the role of police and the importance of maintaining strong police-community relationships.

The following principles attributed to Peel seem to have relevance for a discussion of how body-worn cameras can affect police officers' relationships with community members:

Police must recognize always that the power of the police to fulfill their functions and duties is dependent on public approval of their existence, actions and behavior and on their ability to secure and maintain public respect.

Police must recognize always that to secure and maintain the respect and approval of the public means also the securing of the willing cooperation of the public in the task of securing observance of laws.

Police must maintain at all times a relationship with the public that gives reality to the historic tradition that the police are the public and that the public are the police, the police being only members of the public who are paid to give full time attention to duties which are incumbent on every citizen in the interests of community welfare and existence.*

---

* "Principles of Good Policing," Institute for the Study of Civil Society, http://www.civitas.org.uk/pubs/policeNine.php.

Cameras have also helped assure the public that an agency is serious about transparency and officer accountability, according to several police executives. "We have found that body-worn cameras can actually help strengthen trust and police legitimacy within the community," said Chief of Police Hassan Aden of Greenville, North Carolina. To illustrate this point, Aden shared the following story:

A local community group approached me with a genuine concern that certain officers were racially profiling subjects during traffic stops. We went back and looked at the footage from these officers' body-worn cameras and found that there was indeed a pattern of using flimsy probable cause when making stops. However, we determined that it was a training problem and immediately changed the relevant training protocols. The organization that had raised the complaint was happy with the outcome. They appreciated that we had the body-worn camera footage, that the officers' behavior was investigated, and that we used the video to help us improve.

Securing community support

To mitigate community concerns, many police executives found it useful to engage the community before rolling out their camera programs. The Rialto Police Department, for example, used social media to inform the public about its body-worn camera program. "You have to engage the public before the cameras hit the streets," said Chief Farrar of Rialto. "You have to tell people what the cameras are going to be used for and how everyone can benefit from them."

> *"We want our officers to go out, get out of their cars, and talk to the public about football or whatever it may be to establish an informal relationship. That's how you build partnerships and persuade people to give you information about crime in their area. I think if we say that every single interaction is going to be recorded, the danger is that it will lead to a more officious relationship. Maybe the public will get used to it, just as in our country they've gotten used to cameras on the streets. But as we start off, I think there's a danger that every interaction will become a formal interaction, and the informal relationships may be eroded."*
>
> – Sir Peter Fahy, Chief Constable, Greater Manchester (UK) Police

The Los Angeles Police Department, which is in the process of testing body-worn cameras, plans to solicit public feedback when developing its camera policies. The Greensboro (North Carolina) Police Department partnered with the Greensboro Police Foundation, which launched a "Put Cameras on Cops" public information campaign that included posting billboards and reaching out to the community.

Chief Lanpher of Aberdeen said that it is also important for agencies to engage local policymakers and other stakeholders. "Police departments cannot do this alone," he said. "We went to the mayor, the city council, and the state's attorney's office and showed them actual footage that officers had recorded to demonstrate why these cameras would be useful. Without their support, implementing the program would have been a challenge. Communication and developing those partnerships is critical."

> *"My opinion is that body-worn cameras will help with community relationships. They will show when officers are doing a good job and help us correct when they aren't. This is good for the community."*
>
> — Lieutenant Dan Mark,
> Aurora (Colorado) Police Department

> *"I think it's absolutely critical that we talk to the public about [body-worn cameras]. We need to bring them on board and have them understand what this is about and go through the advantages and disadvantages and the issues."*
>
> – Sir Peter Fahy, Chief Constable,
> Greater Manchester (UK) Police

There are also indications that the public is more accepting of body-worn cameras if agencies are transparent about their camera policies and practices. Some agencies post their camera policies on their websites. In addition, some agencies, such as the Oakland Police Department, have proactively posted body-worn camera footage on their websites to demonstrate transparency and to help resolve questions surrounding controversial incidents.

In Phoenix, the police department released to the media body-worn camera footage from an officer who was fired for misconduct. Assistant Chief of Police Dave Harvey of Phoenix explained that the police union requested the release to demonstrate transparency.

"It is important that agencies are open and transparent with the community," said Deputy Chief Christensen of Fort Collins. "If we only show the good and hide the bad, it will foster distrust of the police."

Protecting intelligence-gathering efforts

In addition to engaging the public to mitigate concerns, some agencies have adopted recording policies that seek to minimize the potential damage that body-worn cameras have on police-community relationships. These agencies limit body-worn camera recordings to calls for service and law enforcement-related contacts, rather than recording every encounter with the public, so that officers do not feel compelled to record the kinds of casual conversations that are central to building informal relationships within the community.

Chief Miller of Topeka said that this approach has worked well. "I recently witnessed a community policing officer having a casual conversation with two citizens," he said. "The officer was wearing a camera, but it was not running at the time. The camera was clearly visible, but it did not create a problem." Chief Miller of Greensboro said, "From a community policing aspect, it does not make sense to record every single interaction with the public. If an officer sees someone on the street and just wants to talk about what is going on in the neighborhood, it is easier to have that conversation if the camera is not running."

A number of agencies also give officers the discretion to turn off their cameras when talking with a person who wants to share information about a crime. This situation can occur when a person approaches an officer with information or if an officer interviews witnesses at a crime scene. In either case, police executives said that officers must weigh the evidentiary value of recording the statement with the reality that some people who share information may not want to talk on camera. "If officers encounter an informant or witness who isn't comfortable being recorded, they have to decide whether obtaining the information outweighs recording the statement," said Lieutenant Rankin of Mesa. "If so, our officers can either turn the camera off or position the camera so that they capture audio but not video. People usually feel more comfortable with just the audio."

Chief Farrar of Rialto said that it is important for officers to maintain credibility with people who might want to share information. "We teach our officers to consider the facts of each incident before they record," he said. "When officers encounter reluctant witnesses, I would suggest that they develop a rapport by being honest and not pressuring them to talk, especially on camera."

Many agencies, while allowing officers to turn off the camera at the request of the person being interviewed, nonetheless strongly encourage officers to record if at all possible. "It is important to remain flexible, as there are no absolutes," said Commander Michael Kurtenbach of Phoenix. "But we would generally recommend an officer to keep the camera on if possible when gathering information from witnesses."

Inspector Danny Inglis of Greater Manchester, United Kingdom, agreed. "I generally think there is more to gain than lose in terms of recording these kinds of statements," he said. "Recording is a way to capture critical intelligence and evidence. Our officers can turn the camera off at the person's request, but they should confirm the reason for this on camera."

The Topeka Police Department takes a similar approach. "Officers should try to leave the camera on to record exactly what a person says. If the person does not want to talk on camera, the officer can turn it off after stating the reason why," said Chief Miller. Again, it is important that officers weigh the situation before making a decision. "The detectives and the prosecutors will want witness interviews on camera if possible. But they would also rather have the good information than have the witness refuse to talk because of the camera," said Miller.

Some police executives said that the decision to record witnesses at a crime scene may depend on whether the scene is live or if it has been controlled. In many places, including Greensboro, Daytona Beach, and Rialto, officers typically leave their cameras running when responding to a live crime scene so they can capture spontaneous statements and impressions. Once the scene has been controlled (crime scene tape is put up, detectives arrive, etc.), it transitions into an investigative scene, and officers can turn the cameras off. Then they can determine whether to record more detailed statements taken from witnesses at the scene.

> *"If officers are talking to a member of the community just to say hello or to ask what is going on in the neighborhood, it is usually better for the relationship if the officer does not record the conversation."*
>
> – Stephen Cullen, Chief Superintendent, New South Wales (AUS) Police Force

> *"We view evidence collection as one of the primary functions of cameras. So in the case of interviewing witnesses, we would make every attempt to capture the statement on video. However, we do allow discretion if the person we approach requests that the camera be turned off. Officers just need to understand what the tradeoff is."*
>
> – Cory Christensen, Deputy Chief of Police, Fort Collins (Colorado) Police Department

Agencies often include protections in their policies to ensure officers do not abuse their recording discretion. If an officer chooses not to record an encounter with someone giving information, he or she must typically document, on camera or in writing, the reason for not recording. In addition, many agencies require officers to activate the camera if an interaction becomes adversarial after the initial contact. Chief Chitwood said this approach has worked in Daytona Beach. "Between their experience and training, the officers know when they need to turn on their cameras. Activating the camera in these situations has become second nature to them," he said.

Lessons learned about impact on community relationships

In their conversations with PERF staff members, police executives and other experts revealed a number of lessons that they have learned when addressing the impact body-worn cameras can have on community relationships:

- Engaging the community prior to implementing a camera program can help secure support for the program and increase the perceived legitimacy of the program in the community.

- Agencies have found it useful to communicate with the public, local policymakers, and other stakeholders about what the cameras will be used for and how the cameras will affect them.

- Social media is an effective way to facilitate public engagement.

- Transparency about the agency's camera policies and practices, both prior to and after implementation, can help increase public acceptance and hold agencies accountable. Examples of transparency include posting policies on the department website and publicly releasing video recordings of controversial incidents.

- Requiring officers to record calls for service and law enforcement-related activities—rather than every encounter with the public—can ensure officers are not compelled to record the types of casual conversations that are central to building informal relationships within the community.

- In cases in which persons are unwilling to share information about a crime if they are being recorded, it is a valuable policy to give officers discretion to deactivate their cameras or to position the camera to record only audio. Officers should consider whether obtaining the information outweighs the potential evidentiary value of capturing the statement on video.

- Recording the events at a live crime scene can help officers capture spontaneous statements and impressions that may be useful in the later investigation or prosecution.

- Requiring officers to document, on camera or in writing, the reasons why they deactivated a camera in situations that they are otherwise required to record promotes officer accountability.

Addressing officer concerns

For a body-worn camera program to be effective, it needs the support not only of the community but also of the frontline officers who will be wearing the cameras. Securing this support can help ensure the legitimacy of a camera program and make its implementation more successful. Agency leaders should engage in ongoing communication with officers about the program's goals, the benefits and challenges of using cameras, and the agency's expectations of the officers.

Officer concerns about body-worn cameras

One of the primary concerns for police executives is the fear that body-worn cameras will erode the trust between officers and the chief and top managers of the department. Some officers may view the cameras as a signal that their supervisors and managers do not trust them, and they worry that supervisors would use the cameras to track and scrutinize their every move. Inspector Inglis of Greater Manchester explained, "I have heard some resentment about the level of scrutiny that officers will be under if they wear body-worn cameras. This is especially true with the first-level response officers, who already feel they are under an extraordinary amount of pressure to get everything right. I can understand this concern."

Given these concerns, one of the most important decisions an agency must make is how it will use camera footage to monitor officer performance. Most agencies permit supervisors to review videos so they can investigate a specific incident or complaint, identify videos for training purposes, ensure the system is working, and monitor overall compliance with the camera program.

However, there is some debate over whether supervisors should also periodically and randomly review videos to monitor officer performance. Some agencies allow periodic monitoring to help proactively identify problems and hold officers accountable for their performance. Other agencies permit periodic monitoring only in certain circumstances, such as when an officer is still in a probationary period or after an officer has received a certain number of complaints. Some agencies prohibit random monitoring altogether because they believe doing so is unnecessary if supervisors conduct reviews when an incident occurs.

"I have heard officers say that while they are not opposed to using body-worn cameras, they do have some concerns. Some of these concerns are more practical, like whether adding new equipment will be overly burdensome. But the larger philosophical concern is whether these cameras send the wrong message about the trust we place in officers. What does it say about officer professionalism and credibility if the department has to arm every officer with a camera?

– Bob Cherry, Detective of
Baltimore Police Department
and President of Baltimore City
Fraternal Order of Police

In Greater Manchester, Inspector Inglis encourages supervisors to randomly review camera footage. "We use random review as a teaching tool, not just a supervision tool," he said. "Supervisors might not get a lot of face time with officers, so reviewing the video is a good way for supervisors to appraise officers and provide feedback. It also helps hold officers accountable and gives them incentive to record."

Other agencies expressly prohibit supervisors from randomly monitoring body-worn camera footage. "Per our policy, we do not randomly review videos to monitor officer performance," said Chief Chitwood of Daytona Beach. "Instead, our review is incident-based, so if there is an issue, we will review the footage. In those cases, we can also review prior videos to see if there is a pattern of behavior."

The Topeka Police Department generally prohibits random monitoring, though supervisors can periodically review videos if officers have received numerous complaints. Chief Miller of Topeka said that this policy strikes a balance between showing trust in the officers and holding them accountable. "If an officer does something wrong, you do not want to be accused of deliberate indifference because you had the videos but ignored them," he said. "You have to show that you reviewed the footage once you had a reason to do so."

Some police officials suggested that an agency's internal audit unit, rather than direct supervisors, should be responsible for periodic, random monitoring. They said this approach allows agencies to monitor compliance with the program and assess officer performance without undermining the trust between an officer and his or her supervisor. These officials stressed that internal audit reviews should be truly random (rather than targeted to a specific officer or officers) and should be conducted in accordance with a written standard of review that is communicated to the officers. Chief of Police Jeff Halstead of Fort Worth, Texas, said, "Random review of the camera footage, either by an internal auditor or a supervisor, is critical to demonstrating that an agency is doing what it is supposed to do and is serious about accountability."

In addition to concerns about trust and supervisor scrutiny, police executives said that some officers worried about the difficulty of operating the cameras and learning a new technology. "Officers can feel inundated with technology," said Chief of Police Roberto Villaseñor of Tucson. "In the past few years, our department has introduced a new records management system and a new digital radio system. So some officers see body-worn cameras as another new piece of technology that they will have to learn." Some officers also said that cameras can be cumbersome and challenging to operate, and agencies often have to test several different camera models and camera placement on the body to determine what works best.

Addressing officer concerns

Agencies have taken various steps to address officer concerns about body-worn cameras. One of the most important steps, according to many police executives, is for agency leaders to engage in open communication with officers about what body-worn cameras will mean for them.

For example, a survey of officers conducted by the Vacaville (California) Police Department found that including officers in the implementation process—and allowing them to provide meaningful input—generated support for the cameras. Some police executives, like Chief Chitwood of Daytona Beach and Chief Lanpher of Aberdeen, have found it useful to attend officer briefings, roll calls, and meetings with union representatives to discuss the camera program. "My staff and I invested considerable time talking at briefings and department meetings with all employees who would be affected by body-worn cameras," said Chief of Police Michael Frazier of Surprise, Arizona. "This has helped us gain support for the program."

> "I think police agencies can help the officer and fulfill their duties to the public by saying, 'We have an officer [whom] we think is having problems, and we are going to look at those videos to determine behavioral patterns.' You do not want to have a problem come up later and claim that you did not know about it even though you had videos. So to me, targeted monitoring makes sense."
>
> – Christy Lopez, Deputy Chief,
> Special Litigation Section,
> Civil Rights Division,
> U.S. Department of Justice

Many police executives said that creating implementation teams comprised of representatives from various units within the department can help improve the legitimacy of a body-worn camera program. For example, as agencies develop body-worn camera policies and protocols, it can be useful to receive input from patrol commanders and officers, investigators, training supervisors, the legal department, communications staff, Internal Affairs personnel, evidence management personnel, and others across the agency who will be involved with body-worn cameras.

Police executives also said it is important to emphasize to officers that body-worn cameras are useful tools that can help them perform their duties. Chief Terry Gainer, U.S. Senate sergeant at arms, believes that framing body-worn cameras as a check on officer behavior is the wrong approach. "It's going to be hard to encourage our officers to be the self-actualized professionals that we want them to be if we say, 'Wear this because we're afraid you're bad, and cameras will help you prove that you're good,'" said Gainer. "Body cameras should be seen as a tool for creating evidence that will help ensure public safety."

Lieutenant John Carli of Vacaville, California, suggests that agencies frame the cameras as a teaching tool, rather than a disciplinary measure, by encouraging supervisors to review footage with officers and provide constructive feedback. One suggestion to accomplish this goal is to highlight officers whose videos demonstrate exemplary performance by showing their footage at training programs or by showing the video during an awards ceremony.

Incremental implementation

Some police executives have also found it helpful to take an incremental approach when implementing body-worn cameras. For example, the San Diego Police Department plans to deploy 100 cameras as part of a pilot program with the eventual goal of outfitting 900 uniformed officers with cameras.

The Greensboro Police Department took a similar approach. "When we first deployed the cameras, there was an undercurrent of apprehension on the part of the officers. So we rolled it out in small increments to help officers get more comfortable with the program," said Chief Miller of Greensboro. Gradual implementation can also help agencies learn which policies, practices, and camera systems are the best fit for their departments. Some agencies, such as the Mesa Police Department, initially assigned cameras to the most tech-savvy officers as a way to ease implementation.

"You have to ask yourself, what is the main reason you are implementing the program? Is it because you want to give officers a helpful tool, or because you do not trust them? The answer to that question—and how you convey it—will influence how officers receive the program."

– Lieutenant John Carli,
Vacaville (California) Police Department

Many agencies have found that officers embrace body-worn cameras when they see evidence of the cameras' benefits. "Our officers have been fairly enthusiastic about body-worn cameras because they have seen examples of how the cameras have cleared fellow officers of complaints," said Lieutenant Dan Mark of Aurora, Colorado. "One officer was threatened by an individual, and it was captured on the officer's camera. We took the footage to the city attorney's office, and the individual was successfully prosecuted. Once that story got out among the officers, we saw a lot more acceptance of the cameras."

Police executives said that in many cases, officers see these benefits once they begin wearing the cameras. "The more officers use the cameras, the more they want to have them," said Lieutenant Gary Lewis from Appleton, Wisconsin. "If I could put cameras on all of my patrol officers, I would have 100 percent support." Chief Farrar of Rialto agreed: "Now that the officers wear the cameras, they say that they could not do without them."

Lessons learned about addressing officer concerns

Police executives revealed a number of lessons about addressing officers' concerns about body-worn cameras:

"At first, officers had a lot of concerns about the 'Big Brother' aspect of body-worn cameras. But once they wear them and see the benefits, they are much more likely to embrace them. Resistance has been almost nonexistent."

– Chris Burbank, Chief of Police,
Salt Lake City (Utah) Police Department

- As with any other deployment of a new technology, program, or strategy, the best approach includes efforts by agency leaders to engage officers on the topic, explain the goals and benefits of the initiative, and address any concerns officers may have.

- Briefings, roll calls, and meetings with union representatives are effective means to communicate information about a body-worn camera program.

- Creating an implementation team that includes representatives from across the department can help strengthen program legitimacy and ease implementation.

- Departments have found that officers support the program if they view the cameras as useful tools: e.g., as a technology that helps to reduce complaints and produce evidence that can be used in court or in internal investigations.

- Recruiting an internal "champion" to help inform officers about the benefits of the cameras has proven successful in addressing officers' hesitation to embrace the new technology.

- Body-worn cameras can serve as a teaching tool when supervisors review footage with officers and provide constructive feedback.

- Taking an incremental approach to implementation can help make deployment run more smoothly. This can include testing cameras during a trial period, rolling out cameras slowly, or initially assigning cameras to tech-savvy officers.

Managing expectations

"In the beginning, some officers were opposed to the cameras. But as they began wearing them, they saw that there were more benefits than drawbacks. Some officers say that they would not go out on the street without a ballistic vest; now they say they will not go out without a camera."

— Lieutenant Harold Rankin,
Mesa (Arizona) Police Department

Police executives said that it has become increasingly common for courts, arbitrators, and civilian review boards to expect police departments to use body-worn cameras. "If your department has a civilian review board, the expectation now is that police should have cameras," said Chief of Police Chris Burbank of Salt Lake City. "If you don't, they will ask, 'Why don't your officers have cameras? Why aren't your cameras fully deployed? Why does the next town over have cameras, but you don't?'"

In addition, people often expect that officers using body-worn cameras will record video of everything that happens while they are on duty. But most police departments do not require officers to record every encounter. Many agencies have policies against recording when it is unsafe or impossible, and some agencies give officers discretion to deactivate their cameras in certain sensitive situations, such as during interviews with victims or witnesses. Camera malfunctions may also occur. Some agencies have taken steps to inform judges, oversight bodies, and the public about these realities of using body-worn cameras.

Police executives said that these expectations can undermine an officer's credibility if questions arise about an incident that was not captured on video. This is one reason why many agencies require officers to articulate, either on camera or in writing, their reasons for turning a camera off in the middle of an incident or for not turning it on in the first place. These issues of credibility are also why it is important to provide rigorous, ongoing officer training on body-worn camera policies and practices. Some agencies find that situational training can be particularly useful. For example, the Oakland Police Department incorporated a program into its police academy that involves officers participating in situational exercises using training model cameras.

"There is a learning curve that comes with using body-worn cameras. And the video cannot always be taken at face value—the full story has to be known before conclusions are reached about what the video shows."

— Major Stephen Willis,
Charlotte-Mecklenburg
(North Carolina) Police Department

Expectations about body-worn cameras can also affect how cases are prosecuted in criminal courts. Some police executives said that judges and juries have come to rely heavily on camera footage as evidence, and some judges have even dismissed a case when video did not exist. "Juries no longer want to hear just officer testimony—they want to see the video," said Detective Cherry of Baltimore. "But the video only gives a small snapshot of events. It does not capture the entire scene, or show the officer's thought process, or show an officer's investigative efforts. This technology shouldn't replace an officer's testimony. I'm concerned that if juries rely only on the video, it reduces the important role that our profession plays in criminal court."

Officer review of video prior to making statements

Given the impact that body-worn cameras can have in criminal and administrative proceedings, there is some question as to whether officers should be allowed to review camera footage prior to making a statement about an incident in which they were involved. According to many police executives, the primary benefit to officer review is that it allows officers to recall events more clearly, which helps get to the truth of what really happened. Some police executives, on the other hand, said that it is better for an officer's statement to reflect what he or she perceived during the event, rather than what the camera footage revealed.

The majority of police executives consulted by PERF are in favor of allowing officers to review body-worn camera footage prior to making a statement about an incident in which they were involved. They believe that this approach provides the best evidence of what actually took place. PERF agrees with this position.

"When you're involved in a tense situation, you don't necessarily see everything that is going on around you, and it can later be difficult to remember exactly what happened," said Police Commissioner Ramsey of Philadelphia. "So I wouldn't have a problem with allowing an officer to review a video prior to making a statement."

Chief Burbank of Salt Lake City agreed. "Officers should be able to review evidence that is gathered about an event, and that includes body-worn camera footage," he said. "Some of the most accurate reports are generated by officers who take a moment to go back and review the circumstances. For example, I was once involved in a pursuit that lasted 30 minutes. I went back and re-drove the route and documented every turn before filing my report. Otherwise, it would have been impossible to remember everything that happened."

Chief Miller of Topeka said that if an officer is not allowed to review video, and if the footage conflicts with the officer's statement, it can create unfair doubts about the officer's credibility. "What we are after is the truth," he said. "If you make a statement that you used force because you thought a suspect had a gun but the video later shows that it was actually a cell phone, it looks like you were lying. But if you truly thought he had a gun, you were not lying—you were just wrong. An officer should be given the chance to make a statement using all of the evidence available; otherwise, it looks like we are just trying to catch an officer in a lie."

"Right from the start, officers now learn how to use the cameras as part of their regular training on patrol procedures. We want activating the cameras to become a muscle memory so that officers do not have to think about it when they are in a real-world situation."

– Sean Whent, Chief of Police, Oakland (California) Police Department

"I tell the officers every day: You usually don't get hurt by the videos you have. What hurts you is when you are supposed to have a video but, for whatever reason, you don't."

– Ron Miller, Chief of Police, Topeka (Kansas) Police Department

Police executives who favor review said that officers will be held accountable for their actions regardless of whether they are allowed to watch the video recordings prior to making a statement. "Officers are going to have to explain their actions, no matter what the video shows," said Chief Burbank of Salt Lake City. Chief Frazier of Surprise, Arizona, said, "If an officer has acted inappropriately, and those actions were recorded, the officer cannot change the record and will have to answer for his or her actions. What will be gained by a review of the video is a more accurate accounting of the incident."

> *The majority of police executives consulted by PERF are in favor of allowing officers to review body-worn camera footage prior to making a statement about an incident in which they were involved.*

Other police executives, however, said that the truth—and the officer's credibility—are better served if an officer is not permitted to review footage of an incident prior to making a statement. "In terms of the officer's statement, what matters is the officer's perspective at the time of the event, not what is in the video," said Major Mark Person of the Prince George's County (Maryland) Police Department. "That perspective is what they are going to have to testify to. If officers watch the video before making a statement, they might tailor the statement to what they see. It can cause them to second-guess themselves, which makes them seem less credible."

Lessons learned about managing expectations

In interviews with PERF staff members, police executives discussed lessons that they have learned for managing expectations about body-worn cameras:

- With more and more agencies adopting body-worn cameras, courts, arbitrators, and civilian review boards have begun to expect not only that agencies will use cameras but also that officers will have footage of everything that happens while they are on duty. If this footage does not exist, even for entirely legitimate reasons, it may impact court or administrative proceedings and create questions about an officer's credibility. Agencies must take steps to manage expectations while also working to ensure that officers adhere to agency policies about activating cameras.

- Educating oversight bodies about the realities of using cameras can help them to understand operational challenges and why there may be situations in which officers are unable to record. This can include demonstrations on how the cameras operate.

- Requiring an officer to articulate, on camera or in writing, the reason for not recording an event can help address questions about missing footage.

- Rigorous, ongoing officer training on body-worn camera policies and protocols is critical for improving camera usage. Situational training in which officers participate in exercises using mock cameras can be particularly useful in helping officers to understand how to operate cameras in the field.

- Many police executives believe that allowing officers to review body-worn camera footage prior to making a statement about an incident in which they were involved provides the best evidence of what actually occurred.

Financial considerations

While body-worn cameras can provide many potential benefits to law enforcement agencies, they come at a considerable financial cost. In addition to the initial purchasing cost, agencies must devote funding and staffing resources toward storing recorded data, managing videos, disclosing copies of videos to the public, providing training to officers, and administering the program.

For some agencies, these costs make it challenging to implement a body-worn camera program. PERF's survey revealed that 39 percent of the respondents that do not use body-worn cameras cited cost as a primary reason. Chief Villaseñor of Tucson said that cost was a major obstacle to getting cameras. "In recent years, we've faced serious budget cuts and have had to reduce staffing levels," he said. "It can be hard to justify spending money on cameras when officers are fighting for their jobs." However, Villaseñor has put together a review committee to evaluate costs and explore how to implement body-worn cameras in Tucson.

Police Commissioner Ramsey said that in departments the size of Philadelphia's, which has 6,500 sworn officers, the cost of implementing a body-worn camera program would be extraordinary. "We've considered using cameras in Philadelphia, and we see all of the benefits they can provide," he said. "Cost is the primary thing holding us back."

Some police executives, however, said that body-worn cameras can save departments money. They said that by improving officer professionalism, defusing potentially confrontational encounters, strengthening officer training, and documenting encounters with the public, body-worn cameras can help reduce spurious lawsuits and complaints against officers. They also said that these savings more than make up for the considerable financial cost of implementing a camera program.

"If there is a lawsuit against the department, the settlements come from the department's operational budget," said Chief Chitwood of Daytona Beach. "By preventing these suits, the department has more money to spend on cars, technology, and other things that benefit officers."[12]

The London Metropolitan Police Service, working together with the College of Policing, is planning to conduct a cost-benefit analysis in conjunction with its upcoming pilot program of 500 cameras. The analysis will measure whether the cameras contribute to cost savings in terms of promoting early guilty pleas in criminal cases and quicker resolution of complaints against officers. The study will also measure community and victim satisfaction with the cameras, as well as how the cameras impact the length of sentences that offenders receive.

> *"I absolutely think that officers should be allowed to review camera footage from an incident in which they were involved, prior to speaking with internal investigators. With what we know of the effect of stressful incidents on the human mind, officers in most instances may not recall every aspect of the incident. Or they may recall events out of sequence or not remember everything until much later. For this reason alone, allowing an officer to review the video prior to making a statement seems prudent."*
>
> – Michael Frazier, Chief of Police, Surprise (Arizona) Police Department

12. See "Perceived Benefits of Body-Worn Cameras" on page 5 for additional discussion of cost-benefit analysis.

Cost of implementation

The price of body-worn cameras currently ranges from approximately $120 to nearly $2,000 for each device. Most of the agencies that PERF consulted spent between $800 and $1,200 for each camera. Prices vary depending on factors such as functionality, storage capacity, and battery life. Agencies must make this initial purchase up front, and sometimes they purchase cameras as part of a contract with the manufacturer for related services, such as data storage and technical assistance.

"Once you put cameras in the field, you're going to amass a lot of data that needs to be stored. Chiefs need to go into this with their eyes wide open. They need to understand what storage is going to cost, what their storage capacities are, and the amount of time it takes to review videos for public release. It is a major challenge."

– Kenton Rainey, Chief of Police, Bay Area Rapid Transit Police Department

Although the initial costs of purchasing the cameras can be steep, many police executives said that data storage is the most expensive aspect of a body-worn camera program. "Data storage costs can be crippling," said Chief Aden of Greenville. Captain Thomas Roberts of Las Vegas agreed. "Storing videos over the long term is an ongoing, extreme cost that agencies have to anticipate," said Roberts.

The cost of data storage will depend on how many videos are produced, how long videos are kept, and where the videos are stored. If the videos are stored on an online cloud database, the costs typically go toward paying a third-party vendor to manage the data and to provide other services, such as technical assistance and forensic auditing. If videos are stored on an in-house server, agencies must often purchase additional computer equipment and spend money on technical staff and systems to ensure the data are secure.

The New Orleans Police Department has launched a plan for deploying 350 body-worn cameras at an anticipated cost of $1.2 million over five years—the bulk of which will go to data storage.[13] One department reported that it will pay $2 million per year, mostly toward data storage, to outfit 900 officers with cameras. Another department spent $67,500 to purchase 50 cameras and will spend approximately $111,000 to store the video on a cloud for two years. In terms of storage, Chief Miller of Topeka said, "I've seen a formula that says that if you have 250 officers that have body-worn cameras, in three years you will produce 2.3 million videos. If the officer was required to run the camera continuously during his or her entire shift, it would produce even more. Managing and storing that data is usually more expensive than buying the cameras."

In addition to the cost of purchasing cameras and storing data, administering a body-worn camera program requires considerable ongoing financial and staffing commitments. Many agencies appoint at least one full-time officer to manage the camera program. Agencies must provide ongoing training programs, ensure that cameras are properly maintained, fix technical problems, and address any issues of officer noncompliance. Some agencies also devote resources toward public information campaigns aimed at educating the community about the program.

According to many police executives, one of the most significant administrative costs—at least in terms of staff resources—involves the process of reviewing and categorizing videos. Although the exact process varies depending on the camera system, officers must typically label, or "tag," videos as evidentiary or non-evidentiary. Evidentiary videos are further categorized according to the type of incident captured in the footage (e.g., homicide, robbery, or traffic citation). This tagging process is critical for determining how a video will be used and how long it will be retained. Most agencies that PERF consulted require officers to download and tag videos by the end of each shift.

---

13. "NOPD Wearable Cameras Expected to Cost $1.2 Million," The Times-Picayune, September 30, 2013, http://www.nola.com/crime/index.ssf/2013/09/post_346.html. Since The Times-Picayune published this article, New Orleans has increased the number of body-worn cameras it expects to deploy from 350 to more than 400.

Some officers have expressed concern about this increase to their administrative workload. "One of the major complaints we heard from officers was that they were spending so much time, after their shifts were over, downloading and tagging their videos," said Commander Tony Filler from Mesa. The department explored several solutions to this problem, ultimately creating an automated process that linked videos to the department's records management system (RMS). The department also purchased from the camera manufacturer electronic tablets that allow officers to view and tag videos while they are in the field. "The tablets were an additional cost, but they were worth it because they save officers a lot of time," said Filler.

Police executives said that there are also significant administrative costs involved with responding to requests from the public or the news media for body-worn camera videos. When an agency receives a disclosure request, often under the Freedom of Information Act, officers or other department personnel must spend time reviewing videos to find the relevant footage, determining whether an exception to the presumption of disclosure applies, identifying portions that by law must be redacted, and performing the redaction process.

Cost-saving strategies

Police executives discussed several strategies that their agencies have employed to mitigate the considerable financial and staffing costs associated with body-worn cameras. These strategies focus primarily on managing the costs of data storage, which many police executives said represent the most expensive aspect of their programs.

Although managing data storage costs is not the primary reason why many agencies have decided against recording non-law enforcement related encounters with the public, it can be a factor. "There is a huge difference in the amount of money it would take to record all encounters versus adopting a more restrictive recording policy," said Chief Miller of Greensboro. "If you record everything, there are going to be astronomical data storage costs. With 500 officers using cameras, we have already produced over 40,000 videos in just seven months. And we would have a lot more if we didn't use a more restrictive recording policy."

Some agencies, such as the police departments in Oakland and Daytona Beach, are working to adopt shorter data retention periods for non-evidentiary footage in an effort to keep data storage costs manageable. Although it is important to keep videos long enough to demonstrate transparency and preserve a record of an encounter, keeping these videos indefinitely would overwhelm an agency's resources. Some agencies may even decide against adopting body-worn cameras due to the extraordinary costs of data storage.

"Responding to public disclosure requests is one of the biggest challenges that my department faces. When a request for a video comes in, an officer has to sit for at least two hours and review the videos to find the footage and identify which portions must by law be redacted. And the actual redactions can take over 10 hours to complete."

– Lieutenant Harold Rankin, Mesa (Arizona) Police Department

"The two biggest challenges that we face in terms of cost are data storage and responding to records requests," said Chief Chitwood of Daytona Beach. "We had to brainstorm about how to address those costs, and one way was through changing our retention times."

As the public becomes more familiar with the existence of police body-worn camera programs, it is reasonable to expect that members of the public and the news media will increasingly want to obtain video recordings. Such public records requests will add to the workload of managing a camera program. Captain James Jones of the Houston Police Department said, "The cost of responding to open records requests played a role when we were deciding how long to keep the video. To protect privacy, you have to go through every video and make sure that you're not disclosing something that you shouldn't. It takes a lot of time, and personnel, to review and redact every tape. If you keep video for five years, it is going to take even more."

Agencies have also explored cheaper storage methods for videos that by law must be retained long-term, such as those containing evidence regarding a homicide or other serious felony. For example, the Greensboro Police Department deletes videos requiring long-term storage from the online cloud after importing them into its RMS or Internal Affairs case management systems. This reduces overall consumption of expensive cloud storage for videos that are required for future court proceedings or long-term retention under state personnel laws. The Charlotte-Mecklenburg Police Department recently completed a body-worn camera trial program, and Major Willis said that the department is exploring alternative storage methods. "Long-term storage costs are definitely going to be a problem. We are looking at cold storage, offline storage, and shorter retention times as a way to keep those costs more manageable," he said.

Many police agencies have also found it useful to conduct a cost-benefit analysis when exploring whether to implement body-worn cameras. For example, agencies can conduct an audit of their claims, judgments, and settlements related to litigation and complaints against officers to determine what costs they may already be incurring. The costs associated with deploying body-worn cameras may be offset by reductions in litigation costs, and agencies should carefully assess their ongoing legal expenses to determine how they could be reduced through the use of body-worn cameras.

Lessons learned about financial considerations

In interviews with PERF staff members, police executives and other experts revealed a number of lessons that they have learned about the financial costs of body-worn cameras:

- The financial and administrative costs associated with body-worn camera programs include costs of the equipment, storing and managing recorded data, and responding to public requests for disclosure.

- It is useful to compare the costs of the camera program with the financial benefits (e.g., fewer lawsuits and unwarranted complaints against officers, as well as more efficient evidence collection).

- Setting shorter retention times for non-evidentiary videos can help make the significant costs of data storage more manageable.

- Videos requiring long-term storage (e.g., those involving serious offenses) can be copied to a disc, attached to the case file, and deleted from the internal server or online cloud. This frees up expensive storage space for videos that are part of an ongoing investigation or that have shorter retention times.

- Linking recorded data to the agency's records management system or using electronic tablets, which officers can use in the field, can ease the administrative burden of tagging and categorizing videos.

The Los Angeles Police Department's Approach to Financing Body-Worn Cameras

In September 2013, Los Angeles Police Commission President Steve Soboroff launched a campaign to raise money to purchase on-body cameras for the Los Angeles Police Department (LAPD). "Before being elected commission president, I heard from numerous leaders in the LAPD that getting on-body cameras was a top priority with a huge upside," said Soboroff in an interview with PERF. "After hearing all of the benefits that this technology could offer, I wanted to find a way to proactively jump-start the project."[*]

Realizing that trying to secure city funds for cameras would be challenging—the LAPD's in-car camera project has been going on for two decades and is only 25 percent complete—Soboroff devised a plan to identify private donors. Within five months, he had raised $1.3 million for a body-worn camera program, exceeding its original goal. Contributors included a number of local companies, executives, and philanthropists, including the Los Angeles Dodgers, movie director Steven Spielberg, entertainment executive Jeffrey Katzenberg, and former Los Angeles Mayor Richard Riordan.[†]

This money will go toward purchasing 600 body-worn cameras for LAPD officers and for video storage, repairs, and other costs over two years.[‡] The LAPD said it would test several camera models before implementing its program.[§] According to Soboroff, the LAPD will eventually need hundreds more cameras to outfit every patrol officer, but he hopes the pilot program will convince city officials that the cameras are worth the money. "I think that the pilot will show that body-worn cameras are transformative. I think it will show so many public safety benefits, and so many savings in litigation settlement dollars, man hours, and attorney hours, that the return on the investment will be apparent and significant," he said.[*]

Soboroff believes that other places can look at the LAPD's fundraising approach as a model. "Probably every city in America has financial concerns. But I believe that there are always going to be local businesses and philanthropists who are willing to help. You just have to show them that there is going to be a positive community and financial return on their investment or donation."[††] However, Soboroff also said it is important that law enforcement agencies retain independence as they develop their programs: "The LAPD has complete control over which cameras it chooses and its camera policies. That is critical—there should be no outside influence from donors."[§§]

As Soboroff indicates, police agencies outside of Los Angeles have also sought private funding for body-worn cameras. For example, the Greensboro (North Carolina) Police Department told PERF that the Greensboro Police Foundation raised $130,000 from private donors to purchase 125 cameras. The Greensboro Police Foundation also created awareness by launching the "Put Cameras on Cops" public information campaign that included reaching out to potential donors and posting billboards in support of the program.

---

[*] Steve Soboroff (president, Los Angeles Police Commission), in discussion with PERF staff members, fall 2013.

[†] "LAPD to Soon Start Testing Body Cameras," *CBS Los Angeles*, January 13, 2014, http://losangeles.cbslocal.com/2014/01/13/lapd-officers-to-soon-start-testing-body-cameras/.

[‡] "LAPD Surpasses Fundraising Goal for Officers' On-Body Cameras," *Los Angeles Times*, November 6, 2013, http://articles.latimes.com/2013/nov/06/local/la-me-ln-lapd-cameras-20131106.

[§] "LAPD to Soon Start Testing Body Cameras."

[**] Soboroff, discussion with PERF staff members.

[††] Ibid.

[§§] Ibid.

Chapter 3. Body-Worn Camera Recommendations

The list of recommendations beginning on page 38 is intended to assist law enforcement agencies as they develop body-worn camera policies and practices. These recommendations, which are based on the research conducted by PERF with support from the COPS Office, reflect the promising practices and lessons that emerged from PERF's September 2013 conference in Washington, D.C., where more than 200 police chiefs, sheriffs, scholars, and federal criminal justice officials shared their experiences with body-worn cameras and their perspectives on the issues discussed in this publication. The recommendations also incorporate feedback gathered during PERF's interviews of more than 40 law enforcement officials and other experts, as well as findings from PERF's review of body-worn camera policies submitted by police agencies across the country.

Each law enforcement agency is different, and what works in one department might not be feasible in another. Agencies may find it necessary to adapt these recommendations to fit their own needs, budget and staffing limitations, state law requirements, and philosophical approach to privacy and policing issues.

When developing body-worn camera policies, PERF recommends that police agencies consult with frontline officers, local unions, the department's legal advisors, prosecutors, community groups, other local stakeholders, and the general public. Incorporating input from these groups will increase the perceived legitimacy of a department's body-worn camera policies and will make the implementation process go more smoothly for agencies that deploy these cameras.

PERF recommends that each agency develop its own comprehensive written policy to govern body-worn camera usage. Policies should cover the following topics:

- Basic camera usage, including who will be assigned to wear the cameras and where on the body the cameras are authorized to be placed

- The designated staff member(s) responsible for ensuring cameras are charged and in proper working order, for reporting and documenting problems with cameras, and for reissuing working cameras to avert malfunction claims if critical footage is not captured

- Recording protocols, including when to activate the camera, when to turn it off, and the types of circumstances in which recording is required, allowed, or prohibited

- The process for downloading recorded data from the camera, including who is responsible for downloading, when data must be downloaded, where data will be stored, and how to safeguard against data tampering or deletion

- The method for documenting chain of custody

- The length of time recorded data will be retained by the agency in various circumstances

- The process and policies for accessing and reviewing recorded data, including the persons authorized to access data and the circumstances in which recorded data can be reviewed

- Policies for releasing recorded data to the public, including protocols regarding redactions and responding to public disclosure requests

- Policies requiring that any contracts with a third-party vendor for cloud storage explicitly state that the videos are owned by the police agency and that its use and access are governed by agency policy

In summary, policies must comply with all existing laws and regulations, including those governing evidence collection and retention, public disclosure of information, and consent. Policies should be specific enough to provide clear and consistent guidance to officers yet allow room for flexibility as the program evolves. Agencies should make the policies available to the public, preferably by posting the policies on the agency website.

General recommendations

1. **Policies should clearly state which personnel are assigned or permitted to wear body-worn cameras and under which circumstances.**

    It is not feasible for PERF to make a specific recommendation about which officers should be required to wear cameras. This decision will depend on an agency's resources, law enforcement needs, and other factors.

    Lessons learned: Some agencies have found it useful to begin deployment with units that have the most frequent contacts with the public (e.g., traffic or patrol officers).

2. **If an agency assigns cameras to officers on a voluntary basis, policies should stipulate any specific conditions under which an officer might be required to wear one.**

    For example, a specified number of complaints against an officer or disciplinary sanctions, or involvement in a particular type of activity (e.g., SWAT operations), might result in an officer being required to use a body-worn camera.

3. **Agencies should not permit personnel to use privately-owned body-worn cameras while on duty.**

    Rationale: Most of the police executives whom PERF interviewed believe that allowing officers to use their own personal cameras while on duty is problematic. PERF agrees with this position. Because the agency would not own the recorded data, there would be little or no protection against the officer tampering with the videos or releasing them to the public or online. In addition, chain-of-custody issues would likely prevent the video evidence from being admitted as evidence in court.

    This recommendation applies regardless of whether the agency has deployed body-worn cameras.

4. **Policies should specify the location on the body on which cameras should be worn.**

   The most appropriate camera placement will depend on several factors, such as the type of camera system used. Agencies should test various camera locations to see what works for their officers in terms of field of vision, comfort, functionality, and ease of use.

   Lessons learned: Police executives have provided feedback regarding their experiences with different camera placements:

   - **Chest:** According to the results of PERF's survey, the chest was the most popular placement location among agencies.

   - **Head/sunglasses:** This is a very popular location because the camera "sees what the officer sees." The downside, however, is that an officer cannot always wear sunglasses. Some officers have also reported that the headband cameras are uncomfortably tight, and some expressed concern about the potential of injury when wearing a camera so close to the eye area.

   - **Shoulder/collar:** Although some officers like the perspective that this placement offers, others have found the camera can too easily be blocked when officers raise their arms. One agency, for example, lost valuable footage of an active shooter incident because the officer's firearm knocked the camera from his shoulder.

   - **Shooting side:** Some agencies specify that officers should wear cameras on the gun/shooting side of the body, which they believe affords a clearer view of events during shooting incidents.

5. **Officers who activate the body-worn camera while on duty should be required to note the existence of the recording in the official incident report.**

   Rationale: This policy ensures that the presence of video footage is accurately documented in the case file so that investigators, prosecutors, oversight boards, and courts are aware of its existence. Prosecutors may need to give potentially exculpatory materials to defense attorneys.

6. **Officers who wear body-worn cameras should be required to articulate on camera or in writing their reasoning if they fail to record an activity that is required by department policy to be recorded. (See recommendations 7–13 for recording protocols.)**

   This may occur, for example, if an officer exercises recording discretion in accordance with the agency's policy because he or she cannot record due to unsafe conditions or if a person does not give consent to record when consent is required.

   Rationale: This holds officers accountable and helps supervisors investigate any recording irregularities that may occur.

Recording protocols

7. **As a general recording policy, officers should be required to activate their body-worn cameras when responding to all calls for service and during all law enforcement-related encounters and activities that occur while the officer is on duty. Exceptions include recommendations 10 and 11 below or other situations in which activating cameras would be unsafe, impossible, or impractical.**

   7a: Policies and training materials should clearly define what is included in the description "law enforcement-related encounters and activities that occur while the officer is on duty." Some agencies have found it useful to provide a list of examples in their policies, such as traffic stops, arrests, searches, interrogations or interviews, and pursuits.

   7b: Officers should also be required to activate the camera during the course of any encounter with the public that becomes adversarial after the initial contact.

   Rationale:

   * The policy affords officers discretion concerning whether to record informal, non-law enforcement-related interactions with members of the community, such as a person asking an officer for directions or officers having casual conversations with people they see on patrol. If officers were always required to record in these situations, it could inhibit the informal relationships that are critical to community policing efforts.

   * The policy can help to secure officer support for a body-worn camera program because it demonstrates to officers that they are trusted to understand when cameras should and should not be activated. Protocols should be reinforced in officer training.

   * The policy is broad enough to capture the encounters and activities that, because they are the most likely to produce evidence or lead to complaints from community members about the police, are most in need of accurate documentation. However, the policy is narrow enough to help keep the amount of recorded data more manageable. This can help reduce the costs associated with storing data, reviewing and tagging data, and responding to public records requests.

8. **Officers should be required to inform subjects when they are being recorded unless doing so would be unsafe, impractical, or impossible.**

   Some states have two-party consent laws that require a person making a recording to obtain the consent of the person or persons being recorded. In this case, officers must obtain consent unless the law provides an exception for police recordings. Most states have one-party consent policies, which allow officers to make recordings without obtaining consent.

   PERF recommends that police in all states inform subjects that they are being recorded, aside from the exceptions stated already. This policy does not mean that officers in one-party consent states must obtain consent prior to recording; rather, they must inform subjects when the camera is running.

   Rationale: The mere knowledge that one is being recorded can help promote civility during police-citizen encounters. Police executives report that cameras improve both officer professionalism and the public's behavior, an observation that is supported by evaluations of body-worn camera programs.

9. Once activated, the body-worn camera should remain in recording mode until the conclusion of an incident/encounter, the officer has left the scene, or a supervisor has authorized (on camera) that a recording may cease.

   Officers should also announce while the camera is recording that the incident has concluded and the recording will now cease.

   See further discussion in recommendation 11b, "Lessons learned."

10. Regardless of the general recording policy contained in recommendation 7, officers should be required to obtain consent prior to recording interviews with crime victims.

    Rationale: There are significant privacy concerns associated with videotaping crime victims. PERF believes that requiring officers to obtain consent prior to recording interviews with victims is the best way to balance privacy concerns with the need to accurately document events.

    This policy should apply regardless of whether consent is required under state law.

    Crime victims should give or deny consent in writing and/or on camera.

11. Regardless of the general recording policy contained in recommendation 7, officers should have the discretion to keep their cameras turned off during conversations with crime witnesses and members of the community who wish to report or discuss criminal activity in their neighborhood.

    11a: When determining whether to record interviews with witnesses and members of the community who wish to share information, officers should always consider both the evidentiary value of recording and the subject's comfort with speaking on camera. To better capture evidence, PERF recommends that officers record statements made by witnesses and people sharing information. However, if a person will not talk unless the camera is turned off, officers may decide that obtaining the information is more important than recording. PERF recommends allowing officers that discretion.

    11b: Policies should provide clear guidance regarding the circumstances under which officers will be allowed to exercise discretion to record, the factors that officers should consider when deciding whether to record, and the process for documenting whether to record.

    Situations in which officers may need to exercise discretion include the following:

    • When a community member approaches an officer to report a crime or share information

    • When an officer attempts to interview witnesses, either at a crime scene or during follow-up interviews

    Rationale: Some witnesses and community members may be hesitant to come forward with information if they know their statements will be recorded. They may fear retaliation, worry about their own privacy, or not feel comfortable sharing sensitive information on camera. This hesitancy can undermine community policing efforts and make it more difficult for officers to collect important information.

Lessons learned: Agencies have adopted various approaches for recording conversations with witnesses or other people who want to share information:

- Record unless the subject requests otherwise; after receiving such a request, the officer can turn the camera off.

- Require officers to proactively obtain consent from the subject prior to recording.

- Allow officers to position the camera so they capture only audio, and not video, of the person making the statement.

- Instruct officers to keep their cameras running during the initial response to an ongoing/live crime scene to capture spontaneous statements and impressions but to turn the camera off once the scene is controlled and moves into the investigative stage. Officers may then make a case-by-case decision about whether to record later interviews with witnesses on the scene.

If an officer does turn the camera off prior to obtaining information from a witness or informant, the officer should document on camera the reason for doing so.

12. **Agencies should prohibit recording other agency personnel during routine, non-enforcement-related activities unless recording is required by a court order or is authorized as part of an administrative or criminal investigation.**

    Under this policy, for example, officers may not record their partner while they are patrolling in their vehicle (unless they are responding to a call for service), are having lunch at their desks, are on breaks, are in the locker room, etc.

    Rationale: This policy supports officer privacy and ensures officers feel safe to engage in routine, informal, non-law enforcement-related conversations with their colleagues.

13. **Policies should clearly state any other types of recordings that are prohibited by the agency.**

    Prohibited recordings should include the following:

    - Conversations with confidential informants and undercover officers (to protect confidentiality and officer safety)

    - Places where a reasonable expectation of privacy exists (e.g., bathrooms or locker rooms)

    - Strip searches

    - Conversations with other agency personnel that involve case tactics or strategy

Download and storage policies

14. **Policies should designate the officer as the person responsible for downloading recorded data from his or her body-worn camera. However, in certain clearly identified circumstances (e.g., officer-involved shootings, in-custody deaths, or other incidents involving the officer that result in a person's bodily harm or death), the officer's supervisor should immediately take physical custody of the camera and should be responsible for downloading the data.**

15. **Policies should include specific measures to prevent data tampering, deleting, and copying.**

    Common strategies include the following:

    - Using data storage systems with built-in audit trails

    - Requiring the supervisor to physically take custody of the officer's body-worn camera at the scene of a shooting or at another serious incident in which the officer was involved and to assume responsibility for downloading the data (see recommendation 14)

    - Conducting forensic reviews of the camera equipment when questions arise (e.g., if an officer claims that he or she failed to record an incident because the camera malfunctioned)

16. **Data should be downloaded from the body-worn camera by the end of each shift in which the camera was used.**

    Rationale: First, many camera systems recharge and clear old data during the downloading process, so this policy helps to ensure cameras are properly maintained and ready for the next use. Second, events will be fresh in the officer's memory for the purpose of tagging and categorizing. Third, this policy ensures evidence will be entered into the system in a timely manner.

17. **Officers should properly categorize and tag body-worn camera videos at the time they are downloaded. Videos should be classified according to the type of event or incident captured in the footage.**

    If video contains footage that can be used in an investigation or captures a confrontational encounter between an officer and a member of the public, it should be deemed "evidentiary" and categorized and tagged according to the type of incident. If the video does not contain evidence or it captures a routine, non-confrontational encounter, it should be considered "non-evidentiary" or a "non-event."

    Rationale: Proper labeling of recorded data is critical for two reasons. First, the retention time for recorded data typically depends on the category of the event captured in the video. Thus, proper tagging is critical for determining how long the data will be retained in the agency's system. Second, accurate tagging helps supervisors, prosecutors, and other authorized personnel to readily identify and access the data they need for investigations or court proceedings.

    Lessons learned: Some agencies report that reviewing and tagging recorded data can be a time-consuming process that is prone to human error. One agency addressed this issue by working with the camera manufacturer to develop an automated process that links the recorded data to the agency's records management system. Some camera systems can also be linked to electronic tablets that officers can use to review and tag recorded data while still in the field.

18. **Policies should specifically state the length of time that recorded data must be retained. For example, many agencies provide 60-day or 90-day retention times for non-evidentiary data.**

Agencies should clearly state all retention times in the policy and make the retention times public by posting them on their websites to ensure community members are aware of the amount of time they have to request copies of video footage.

Retention times for recorded data are typically subject to state laws and regulations that govern other types of evidence. Agencies should consult with legal counsel to ensure retention policies are in compliance with these laws.

- For evidentiary data, most state laws provide specific retention times depending on the type of incident. Agencies should set retention times for recorded data to meet the minimum time required by law but may decide to keep recorded data longer.

- For non-evidentiary data, policies should follow state law requirements when applicable. However, if the law does not provide specific requirements for non-evidentiary data, the agency should set a retention time that takes into account the following:

  o Departmental policies governing retention of other types of electronic records

  o Openness of the state's public disclosure laws

  o Need to preserve footage to promote transparency and investigate citizen complaints

  o Capacity for data storage

Agencies should obtain written approval for retention schedules from their legal counsel and prosecutors.

19. **Policies should clearly state where body-worn camera videos are to be stored.**

The decision of where to store recorded data will depend on each agency's needs and resources. PERF does not recommend any particular storage method. Agencies should consult with their department's legal counsel and with prosecutors to ensure the method for data storage meets any legal requirements and chain-of-custody needs.

Common storage locations include in-house servers (managed internally) and online cloud databases (managed by a third-party vendor). Some agencies burn recorded data to discs as part of the evidence file folder.

Lessons learned: Factors that agency leaders should consider when determining storage location include the following:

- Security concerns

- Reliable methods for backing up data

- Chain-of-custody issues

- Capacity for data storage

Lessons learned: Police executives and prosecutors report that they have had no issues to date with using a third-party vendor to manage recorded data on an online cloud, so long as the chain of custody can be properly established. When using a third-party vendor, the keys to protecting the security and integrity of the data include the following:

- Using a reputable, experienced third-party vendor

- Entering into a legal contract that governs the vendor relationship and protects the agency's data

- Using a system that has a built-in audit trail to prevent data tampering and unauthorized access

- Using a system that has a reliable method for automatically backing up data

- Consulting with prosecutors and legal advisors

Recorded data access and review

20. **Officers should be permitted to review video footage of an incident in which they were involved, prior to making a statement about the incident.**

    This can occur, for example, if an officer is involved in a shooting and has to give a statement about the shooting that may be used in an administrative review or a criminal or civil court proceeding.

    Rationale:

    - Reviewing footage will help officers remember the incident more clearly, which leads to more accurate documentation of events. The goal is to find the truth, which is facilitated by letting officers have all possible evidence of the event.

    - Real-time recording of the event is considered best evidence. It often provides a more accurate record than an officer's recollection, which can be affected by stress and other factors. Research into eyewitness testimony demonstrates that stressful situations with many distractions are difficult even for trained observers to recall correctly.

    - If a jury or administrative review body sees that the report says one thing and the video indicates another, this can create inconsistencies in the evidence that might damage a case or unfairly undermine the officer's credibility.

21. **Written policies should clearly describe the circumstances in which supervisors will be authorized to review an officer's body-worn camera footage.**

    Common situations in which supervisors may need to review footage include the following:

    - To investigate a complaint against an officer or a specific incident in which the officer was involved

    - To identify videos for training purposes and for instructional use

PERF also recommends that supervisors be permitted to review footage to ensure compliance with recording policies and protocols, specifically for the following situations:

- When officers are still in a probationary period or are with a field training officer

- When officers have had a pattern of allegations of verbal or physical abuse

- When officers, as a condition of being put back on the street, agree to a more intensive review

- When officers are identified through an early intervention system

22. **An agency's internal audit unit, rather than the officer's direct chain of command, should periodically conduct a random review of body-worn camera footage to monitor compliance with the program and assess overall officer performance.**

    Rationale: PERF recommends that an agency's internal audit unit (e.g., the Staff Inspection Unit) conduct these random footage reviews to avoid undermining the trust between an officer and his or her supervisor.

    The internal audit unit's random monitoring program should be governed by a clearly-defined policy, which should be made available to officers.

23. **Policies should explicitly forbid agency personnel from accessing recorded data for personal use and from uploading recorded data onto public and social media websites.**

    Rationale: Agencies must take every possible precaution to ensure body-worn camera footage is not used, accessed, or released for any unauthorized purpose. This prohibition should be explicitly stated in the written policy.

    Written policies should also describe the sanctions for violating this prohibition.

24. **Policies should include specific measures for preventing unauthorized access or release of recorded data.**

    Some systems have built-in audit trails. All video recordings should be considered the agency's property and be subject to any evidentiary laws and regulations.

25. **Agencies should have clear and consistent protocols for releasing recorded data externally to the public and the news media (a.k.a. Public Disclosure Policies). Each agency's policy must be in compliance with the state's public disclosure laws (often known as Freedom of Information Acts).**

    Policies should state who is allowed to authorize the release of data and the process for responding to public requests for data. PERF generally recommends a broad disclosure policy to promote agency transparency and accountability.

    However, there are some videos—such as recordings of victims and witnesses and videos taken inside private homes—that raise privacy concerns if they are publicly released. These privacy considerations must be taken into account when deciding when to release video to the public. The policy should also identify any exemptions to public disclosure that are outlined in the state Freedom of Information laws.

In certain cases, an agency may want to proactively release body-worn camera footage. For example, some agencies have released footage to share what the officer's video camera showed regarding controversial incidents. In some cases, the video may support a contention that an officer was in compliance with the law. In other cases, the video may show that the department is taking appropriate action against an officer. Policies should specify the circumstances in which this type of public release is allowed. When determining whether to proactively release data to the public, agencies should consider whether the footage will be used in a criminal court case, and the potential effects that releasing the data might have on the case.

Lessons learned:

● While agencies that have implemented body-worn cameras report that responding to public disclosure requests can be administratively complicated, departments must implement systems that ensure responses to these requests are timely, efficient, and fully transparent. This process should include reviewing footage to locate the requested video, determining which portions are subject to public release under state disclosure laws, and redacting any portions that state law prohibits from disclosure (e.g., images of juveniles' faces).

● The most important element of an agency's policy is to communicate it clearly and consistently within the community.

Training policies

26. **Body-worn camera training should be required for all agency personnel who may use or otherwise be involved with body-worn cameras.**

    This should include supervisors whose officers wear cameras, records/evidence management personnel, training personnel, Internal Affairs, etc.

    Agencies may also wish to offer training as a courtesy to prosecutors to help them better understand how to access the data (if authorized), what the limitations of the technology are, and how the data may be used in court.

27. **Before agency personnel are equipped with body-worn cameras, they must receive all mandated training.**

28. **Body-worn camera training should include the following:**

    ● All practices and protocols covered by the agency's body-worn camera policy (which should be distributed to all personnel during training)

    ● An overview of relevant state laws governing consent, evidence, privacy, and public disclosure

    ● Procedures for operating the equipment safely and effectively

    ● Scenario-based exercises that replicate situations that officers might encounter in the field

- Procedures for downloading and tagging recorded data

- Procedures for accessing and reviewing recorded data (only for personnel authorized to access the data)

- Procedures for preparing and presenting digital evidence for court

- Procedures for documenting and reporting any malfunctioning device or supporting system

29. **A body-worn camera training manual should be created in both digital and hard-copy form and should be readily available at all times to agency personnel.**

    The training manual should be posted on the agency's intranet.

30. **Agencies should require refresher courses on body-worn camera usage and protocols at least once per year.**

    Agencies should also require ongoing monitoring of body-worn camera technology for updates on equipment, data storage options, court proceedings, liability issues, etc.

Policy and program evaluation

31. **Agencies should collect statistical data concerning body-worn camera usage, including when video footage is used in criminal prosecutions and internal affairs matters.**

    Statistics should be publicly released at various specified points throughout the year or as part of the agency's year-end report.

    Rationale: Collecting and releasing statistical information about body-worn camera footage helps to promote transparency and trust within the community. It also allows agencies to evaluate the effectiveness of their body-worn camera programs and to identify areas for improvement.

32. **Agencies should conduct evaluations to analyze the financial impact of implementing a body-worn camera program.**

    These studies should analyze the following:

    - The anticipated or actual cost of purchasing equipment, storing recorded data, and responding to public disclosure requests

    - The anticipated or actual cost savings, including legal fees and other costs associated with defending lawsuits and complaints against officers

    - Potential funding sources for a body-worn camera program

33. Agencies should conduct periodic reviews of their body-worn camera policies and protocols.

Evaluations should be based on a set standard of criteria, such as the following:

- Recording policies

- Data storage, retention, and disclosure policies

- Training programs

- Community feedback

- Officer feedback

- Internal audit review discoveries

- Any other policies that govern body-worn camera usage

An initial evaluation should be conducted at the conclusion of the body-worn camera pilot program or at a set period of time (e.g., six months) after the cameras were first implemented. Subsequent evaluations should be performed on a regular basis as determined by the agency.

Rationale: Body-worn camera technology is new and evolving. In addition, the policy issues associated with body-worn cameras are just recently being fully considered and understood. Agencies must continue to examine whether their policies and protocols take into account new technologies, are in compliance with new laws, and reflect the most up-to-date research and best practices. Evaluations will also help agencies determine whether their policies and practices are effective and appropriate for their departments.

Conclusion

The recent emergence of body-worn cameras has already impacted policing, and this impact will increase as more agencies adopt this technology. Police agencies that are considering implementing body-worn cameras should not enter into this decision lightly. Once an agency travels down the road of deploying body-worn cameras, it will be difficult to reverse course because the public will come to expect the availability of video records.

When implemented correctly, body-worn cameras can help strengthen the policing profession. These cameras can help promote agency accountability and transparency, and they can be useful tools for increasing officer professionalism, improving officer training, preserving evidence, and documenting encounters with the public. However, they also raise issues as a practical matter and at the policy level, both of which agencies must thoughtfully examine. Police agencies must determine what adopting body-worn cameras will mean in terms of police-community relationships, privacy, trust and legitimacy, and internal procedural justice for officers.

Police agencies should adopt an incremental approach to implementing a body-worn camera program. This means testing the cameras in pilot programs and engaging officers and the community during implementation. It also means carefully crafting body-worn camera policies that balance accountability, transparency, and privacy rights, as well as preserving the important relationships that exist between officers and members of the community.

PERF's recommendations provide guidance that is grounded in current research and in the lessons learned from police agencies that have adopted body-worn cameras. However, because the technology is so new, a large body of research does not yet exist regarding the effects body-worn cameras have on policing. Additional research and field experience are needed before the full impact of body-worn cameras can be understood, and PERF's recommendations may evolve as further evidence is gathered.

Like other new forms of technology, body-worn cameras have the potential to transform the field of policing. To make sure this change is positive, police agencies must think critically about the issues that cameras raise and must give careful consideration when developing body-worn camera policies and practices. First and foremost, agencies must always remember that the ultimate purpose of these cameras should be to help officers protect and serve the people in their communities.

Appendix A. Recommendations Matrix

The tables below include the 33 policy recommendations and other lessons learned that are found throughout this publication. These recommendations, which are based on the research conducted by PERF with support from the COPS Office, reflect the promising practices and lessons that emerged from PERF's September 2013 conference in Washington, D.C., where more than 200 police chiefs, sheriffs, scholars, and federal criminal justice officials shared their experiences with body-worn cameras and their perspectives on the issues discussed in this report. The recommendations also incorporate feedback gathered during PERF's interviews of more than 40 law enforcement officials and other experts, as well as findings from PERF's review of body-worn camera policies submitted by police agencies across the country.

Policy recommendations

General recommendations

No.	Recommendation	Rationale for Recommendation and Tips for Implementation	Page Reference(s)
1	Policies should clearly state which personnel are assigned or permitted to wear body-worn cameras and under which circumstances.	The decision about which officers should wear body-worn cameras will depend on an agency's resources, law enforcement needs, and other factors. Implementation tip: • Some agencies find it useful to begin deployment with units that have the most frequent contacts with the public (e.g., traffic or patrol officers).	Assignment of cameras: p. 38 Incremental implementation: p. 27
2	If an agency assigns cameras to officers on a voluntary basis, policies should stipulate any specific conditions under which an officer might be required to wear one.	Officers who are not otherwise assigned body-worn cameras may become required to wear one in certain circumstances, such as the following: • After receiving a specified number of complaints or disciplinary actions • When participating in a certain type of activity, such as SWAT operations	Use of body-worn cameras to improve officer performance: p. 7–9 Assignment of cameras: p. 38
3	Agencies should not permit personnel to use privately-owned body-worn cameras while on duty.	The agency would not own recordings made from personal devices; thus, there would be little or no protection against data tampering or releasing the videos to the public or online. There would also be chain-of-custody issues with admitting personal recordings as evidence in court.	Personal cameras: p. 38 Data protection: pp. 15–16; 17–19; 42–47
4	Policies should specify the location on the body on which cameras should be worn.	Implementation tips: • Factors to consider when determining camera placement include field of vision, comfort, functionality, ease of use, and the type of camera system used. • Agencies should field test various camera locations.	Camera placement: p. 39

No.	Recommendation	Rationale for Recommendation and Tips for Implementation	Page Reference(s)
5	Officers who activate the body-worn camera while on duty should be required to note the existence of the recording in the official incident report.	This policy ensures that the presence of video footage is accurately documented in the case file so that investigators, prosecutors, oversight boards, and courts are aware of its existence.	Documentation of camera usage: p. 39
6	Officers who wear body-worn cameras should be required to articulate on camera or in writing their reasoning if they fail to record an activity that is required by department policy to be recorded. (See Recommendations 7-13 for Recording Protocols.)	There may be times when an officer fails to record an event or activity that is otherwise required by agency policy to be recorded. This may arise under the following circumstances: • When conditions make it unsafe or impossible to activate the camera • When an officer exercises discretion, per agency policy, to not record because doing so would be detrimental to other agency priorities (e.g., protecting privacy rights, preserving community relations, or facilitating intelligence gathering) • When the camera malfunctions or otherwise fails to capture the event/activity In these situations, officers should document in writing and/or on camera their reasons for not recording. This holds officers accountable, allows supervisors to investigate recording irregularities, and documents the absence of video footage for investigations and court proceedings. Implementation tips: • The failure to record should be noted in the officer's written report. • If the officer deactivates the camera in the middle of recording, the officer should state on camera the reasons why.	Documenting the failure to record: pp. 13; 14; 18–19; 23; 28; 30; 39 Recording discretion: pp. 12–14; 18–19; 22–23; 40

Recording protocols

No.	Recommendation	Findings in Support of Recommendation and Tips for Implementation	Page Reference(s)
7	General recording policy: Officers should be required to activate their body-worn cameras when responding to all calls for service and during all law enforcement-related encounters and activities that occur while the officer is on duty. Exceptions include recommendations 10 and 11 below or other situations in which activating cameras would be unsafe, impossible, or impractical.	Rather than requiring officers to record all encounters with the public, most agencies that PERF consulted require officers to record during calls for service and during all law enforcement-related encounters and activities. PERF agrees with this approach. This means that officers have discretion whether to record informal, non-law enforcement-related interactions with the public. The reasons for adopting this approach include the following: • Protecting relationships between the police and the community • Promoting community policing efforts • Securing officer support for the body-worn camera program by signaling that they are trusted to know when to record • Keeping data storage manageable	Recording discretion: pp. 12–14; 18–19; 22–23; 40
7a	Policies and training materials should clearly define what is included in the description "law enforcement-related encounters and activities that occur while the officer is on duty."	Officers should have clear guidance about which specific types of activities, events, and encounters they are required to record. Implementation tip: • Some agencies have found it useful to provide a list of specific examples in their policies, such as traffic stops, arrests, searches, interrogations or interviews, and pursuits. Policies should note that these types of lists are not exhaustive. • These recording policies should be reinforced in training.	Recording guidance: pp. 13; 18–24; 40
7b	Officers should also be required to activate the camera during the course of **any** encounter with the public that becomes adversarial after the initial contact.	If officers are given discretion to not record informal, non-law enforcement-related encounters with the public, they should nonetheless be instructed to activate their cameras if the encounter becomes adversarial. This provides documentation of the encounter in the event that a complaint later arises. It also may help to defuse tense situations and prevent further escalation. Implementation tip: • Officers may be called upon to activate their cameras quickly and in high-stress situations. Therefore, training programs should strive to ensure that camera activation becomes second-nature to officers. Situational training is particularly useful to achieve this goal.	Recording adversarial encounters: pp. 23; 40 Preserving documentation for complaints: pp. 5–7 Situational training: pp. 28–29; 47

No.	Recommendation	Findings in Support of Recommendation and Tips for Implementation	Page Reference(s)
8	Officers should be required to inform subjects when they are being recorded unless doing so would be unsafe, impractical, or impossible.	The mere knowledge that one is being recorded can help promote civility during police encounters with the public. Many police executives have found that officers can avoid adversarial situations if they inform people that they are being recorded. Implementation tips: • In states with two-party consent laws, officers are required to announce they are recording and to obtain the subject's consent. Agencies should consult their state laws to determine whether this requirement applies. • In one-party consent states, PERF's recommendation that officers inform a person that he or she is being recorded does *not* mean that officers must also obtain the person's consent to record. • An officer may exercise discretion to not announce that he or she is recording if doing so would be unsafe, impractical, or impossible.	Consent (in general): pp. 14; 40 Improving police-citizen encounters: pp. 6; 14 Informing when recording: pp. 6; 14; 18–19; 40
9	Once activated, the body-worn camera should remain in recording mode until the conclusion of an incident/encounter, the officer has left the scene, or a supervisor has authorized (on camera) that a recording may cease.	Implementation tip: • Prior to deactivating the camera, officers should announce that the incident has concluded and that the recording will now cease.	Camera deactivation: pp. 18–19; 41
10	Regardless of the general recording policy contained in recommendation 7, officers should be required to obtain consent prior to recording interviews with crime victims.	There are significant privacy concerns associated with videotaping crime victims. PERF believes that requiring officers to obtain consent prior to recording interviews with victims is the best way to balance privacy concerns with the need to accurately document events. Implementation tips: • Victims should give or deny consent in writing and/ or on camera. • This policy should apply regardless of whether consent is required under state law.	Recording crime victims: pp. 13; 18–19; 40-41

No.	Recommendation	Findings in Support of Recommendation and Tips for Implementation	Page Reference(s)
11	Regardless of the general recording policy contained in recommendation 7, officers should have the discretion to keep their cameras turned off during conversations with crime witnesses and members of the community who wish to report or discuss criminal activity in their neighborhood.	One of the most important jobs of police officers is to gather information about crime that occurs in their communities. These intelligence-gathering efforts may be formal (e.g., through interviews with witnesses of a crime) or informal (e.g., through conversations with community members with whom the officer has a relationship). Some police executives report that body-worn cameras can inhibit intelligence-gathering efforts, as some witnesses and community members may be hesitant to report information if they know their statements will be recorded. They may fear retaliation, worry about their own privacy, or not feel comfortable sharing sensitive information on camera. Officers should have the discretion to keep their cameras turned off in these situations. Implementation tips: • If a person is not comfortable sharing information on camera, some agencies permit officers to position the camera so that they capture only audio, not video, recordings of the person making the statement. This affords greater privacy protections while still preserving evidentiary documentation. • It is useful for officers to keep their cameras running during the initial response to an ongoing/live crime scene to capture spontaneous statements and impressions made by people at the scene. Once the scene is controlled and has moved into the investigative stage, officers may make a case-by-case decision about whether to record later interviews with witnesses. • When encountering a reluctant witness, officers should attempt to develop a rapport by being honest and not pressuring the person to talk on camera. • If an officer turns the camera off prior to obtaining information, the officer should document on camera the reason for doing so.	Impact on intelligence-gathering efforts: pp. 19–21 Recording statements from witnesses or citizen informants: pp. 22–23; 41–42
11a	When determining whether to record interviews with witnesses and members of the community who wish to share information, officers should always consider both the evidentiary value of recording and the subject's comfort with speaking on camera. To better capture evidence, PERF recommends that officers record statements made by witnesses and people sharing information. However, if a person will not talk unless the camera is turned off, officers may decide that obtaining the information is more important than recording. PERF recommends allowing officers that discretion.	Recorded statements made by crime victims and members of the community can provide valuable evidence for investigations and prosecutions. Therefore, it is always preferable to capture these statements on camera when possible. Implementation tips: • Many agencies instruct officers to keep the camera activated when speaking with witnesses or informants unless the person actively requests otherwise. • Agencies should work with prosecutors to determine how best to weigh the importance of having a recorded statement versus the importance of gathering information when a witness refuses to speak on camera.	Recording statements from witnesses or citizen informants: pp. 22–23; 41–42
11b	Policies should provide clear guidance regarding the circumstances under which officers will be allowed to exercise discretion to record, the factors that officers should consider when deciding whether to record, and the process for documenting whether to record.	Although discretion is important for protecting community policing efforts, this discretion must not be unlimited. Officers should always adhere to agency policies regarding discretion and should document when they exercise this discretion.	Recording statements from witnesses or citizen informants: pp. 22–23; 41–42

No.	Recommendation	Findings in Support of Recommendation and Tips for Implementation	Page Reference(s)
12	Agencies should prohibit recording other agency personnel during routine, non-enforcement-related activities unless recording is required by a court order or is authorized as part of an administrative or criminal investigation.	This policy supports officer privacy and ensures officers feel safe to engage in routine, informal, non-law enforcement-related conversations with their colleagues. Situations that should not be recorded include the following: • Non-law enforcement-related conversations held between officers while on patrol (except while responding to a call for service) • Conversations between agency personnel held during breaks, at lunch, in the locker room, or during other non-law enforcement-related activities	Prohibited recordings: p. 42
13	Policies should clearly state any other types of recordings that are prohibited by the agency. Prohibited recordings should include the following: • Conversations with confidential informants and undercover officers to protect confidentiality and officer safety • Places where a reasonable expectation of privacy exists (e.g., bathrooms or locker rooms) • Strip searches • Conversations with other agency personnel that involve case tactics or strategy	When determining whether a recording should be prohibited, agencies should consider privacy concerns, the need for transparency and accountability, the safety of the officer and the citizen, and the evidentiary value of recording.	Prohibited recordings: pp. 37–38; 42 Privacy considerations (in general): pp. 11–20

Download and storage policies

No.	Recommendation	Findings in Support of Recommendation and Tips for Implementation	Page Reference(s)
14	Policies should designate the officer as the person responsible for downloading recorded data from his or her body-worn camera. However, in certain clearly identified circumstances (e.g., officer-involved shootings, in-custody deaths, or other incidents involving the officer that result in a person's bodily harm or death), the officer's supervisor should immediately take physical custody of the camera and should be responsible for downloading the data.	In most cases, it is more efficient for an officer to download recorded data from his or her own body-worn camera. The officer will have the best access to the camera and knowledge of the footage for tagging/documentation purposes. However, if the officer is involved in a shooting or other incident that results in someone's bodily harm or death, it is prudent for the officer's supervisor to take immediate custody of the officer's camera for evidence preservation purposes.	Data protection: pp. 15–16; 18–19; 42–44
15	Policies should include specific measures to prevent data tampering, deleting, and copying.	Implementation tips: • Agencies should create an audit system that monitors who accesses recorded data, when, and for what purpose. Some camera systems come with a built-in audit trail. • Agencies can conduct forensic reviews to determine whether recorded data has been tampered with.	Data protection: pp. 15–16; 18–19; 42–45
16	Data should be downloaded from the body-worn camera by the end of each shift in which the camera was used.	The majority of agencies that PERF consulted require officers to download recorded data by the conclusion of his or her shift. The reasons for this include the following: • Many camera systems recharge and clear old data during the downloading process. • Events will be fresh in the officer's memory for the purpose of tagging and categorizing. • Evidence will be entered into the system in a timely manner.	Data protection: pp. 15–16; 18–19; 42–45
17	Officers should properly categorize and tag body-worn camera videos at the time they are downloaded. Videos should be classified according to the type of event or incident captured in the footage.	Properly categorizing and labeling/tagging recorded video is important for the following reasons: • The type of event/incident on the video will typically dictate data retention times. • It enables supervisors, investigators, and prosecutors to more easily identify and access the data they need. Implementation tips: • Some camera systems can be linked to an agency's records management system to allow for automated tagging and documentation. • Some camera systems can be linked to electronic tablets that officers can use to review and tag recorded data while in the field. This saves the officer time spent tagging data at the end of his or her shift.	Data tagging: pp. 16–17; 18–19; 33–34; 43

No.	Recommendation	Findings in Support of Recommendation and Tips for Implementation	Page Reference(s)
18	Policies should specifically state the length of time that recorded data must be retained. For example, many agencies provide 60-day or 90-day retention times for non-evidentiary data.	Most state laws provide specific retention times for videos that contain evidentiary footage that may be used for investigations and court proceedings. These retention times will depend on the type of incident captured in the footage. Agencies typically have more discretion when setting retention times for videos that do not contain evidentiary footage. When setting retention times, agencies should consider the following: • State laws governing evidence retention • Departmental policies governing retention of other types of electronic records • The openness of the state's public disclosure laws • The need to preserve footage to promote transparency • The length of time typically needed to receive and investigate citizen complaints • The agency's capacity for data storage Implementation tips: • Agencies should make retention times public by posting them on their websites. • When setting retention times, agencies should consult with legal counsel to ensure compliance with relevant evidentiary laws. Agencies should obtain written approval for retention schedules from prosecutors and legal counsel.	Data retention: pp. 16–19; 33–34; 43–45

No.	Recommendation	Findings in Support of Recommendation and Tips for Implementation	Page Reference(s)
19	Policies should clearly state where body-worn camera videos are to be stored.	Common storage locations include in-house servers (managed internally) and online cloud databases (managed by a third-party vendor). Factors that agencies should consider when determining where to store data include the following: • Security concerns • Reliable methods for backing up data • Chain-of-custody issues • Capacity for data storage Implementation tips: • Agencies should consult with prosecutors and legal advisors to ensure data storage methods meet all legal requirements and chain-of-custody needs. • For videos requiring long-term storage, some agencies burn the data to a disc, attach it to the case file, and delete it from the internal server or online database. This frees up expensive storage space for videos that are part of an ongoing investigation or that have shorter retention times. • The agencies that PERF consulted report having no issues to date with using a third-party vendor to manage recorded data. To protect the security and integrity of data managed by a third party, agencies should use a reputable, experienced vendor; enter into a legal contract with the vendor that protects the agency's data; ensure the system includes a built-in audit trail and reliable backup methods; and consult with legal advisors.	Data storage: pp. 15–16; 18–19; 32–34; 43–44

Recorded data access and review

No.	Recommendation	Findings in Support of Recommendation and Tips for Implementation	Page Reference(s)
20	Officers should be permitted to review video footage of an incident in which they were involved, prior to making a statement about the incident.	Most agencies that PERF consulted permit officers to review video footage of an incident in which they were involved, such as a shooting, prior to making a statement that might be used in an administrative review or court proceeding. The reasons for this policy include the following: • Reviewing footage will help lead to the truth of the incident by helping officers to remember an incident more clearly. • Real-time recording is considered best evidence and provides a more accurate record than the officer's recollection. • Research into eyewitness testimony has demonstrated that stressful situations with many distractions are difficult for even trained observers to recall correctly. • Officers will have to explain and account for their actions, regardless of what the video shows.	Officer review of footage: pp. 29–30; 45–47
21	Written policies should clearly describe the circumstances in which supervisors will be authorized to review an officer's body-worn camera footage.	PERF recommends that supervisors be authorized to review footage in the following circumstances: • When a supervisor needs to investigate a complaint against an officer or a specific incident in which the officer was involved • When a supervisor needs to identify videos for training purposes and for instructional use • When officers are still in a probationary period or are with a field training officer • When officers have had a pattern of allegations of abuse or misconduct • When officers have agreed to a more intensive review as a condition of being put back on the street • When an officer has been identified through an early intervention system	Supervisor review of footage: pp. 24–26; 27–28; 45–47

No.	Recommendation	Findings in Support of Recommendation and Tips for Implementation	Page Reference(s)
22	An agency's internal audit unit, rather than the officer's direct chain of command, should periodically conduct a random review of body-worn camera footage to monitor compliance with the program and assess overall officer performance.	Randomly monitoring an officer's camera footage can help proactively identify problems, determine noncompliance, and demonstrate accountability. However, unless prompted by one of the situations described in recommendation 21, PERF does not generally recommend that supervisors randomly monitor footage recorded by officers in their chain of command for the purpose of spot-checking the officers' performance. Instead, an agency's internal audit unit should be responsible for conducting random monitoring. This allows agencies to monitor compliance with the program and assess performance without undermining the trust between an officer and his or her supervisor. Implementation tips: • Internal audit reviews should be truly random and not target a specific officer or officers. • Audits should be conducted in accordance with a written standard of review that is communicated to officers.	Internal audit unit review of footage: pp. 24–26; 28; 45–47
23	Policies should explicitly forbid agency personnel from accessing recorded data for personal use and from uploading recorded data onto public and social media websites.	Agencies must take every possible precaution to ensure that camera footage is not used, accessed, or released for any unauthorized purposes. Implementation tips: • Written policies should describe the sanctions for violating this prohibition.	Data protection: pp. 15–16; 18–19; 45–46
24	Policies should include specific measures for preventing unauthorized access or release of recorded data.	All video recordings should be considered the agency's property and be subject to any evidentiary laws and regulations. (See also recommendations 15 and 23.)	Data protection: pp. 15–16; 18–19; 45–46

No.	Recommendation	Findings in Support of Recommendation and Tips for Implementation	Page Reference(s)
25	Agencies should have clear and consistent protocols for releasing recorded data externally to the public and the news media (a.k.a. Public Disclosure Policies). Each agency's policy must be in compliance with the state's public disclosure laws (often known as Freedom of Information Acts).	PERF generally recommends a broad public disclosure policy for body-worn camera videos. By implementing a body-worn camera program, agencies are demonstrating that they are committed to transparency and accountability, and their disclosure policies should reflect this commitment. However, there are some situations when an agency may determine that publicly releasing body-worn camera footage is not appropriate. These include the following: • Videos that contain evidentiary footage being used in an ongoing investigation or court proceeding are typically exempted from disclosure by state public disclosure laws. • When the videos raise privacy concerns, such as recordings of crime victims or witnesses or footage taken inside a private home, agencies must balance privacy concerns against the need for transparency while complying with relevant state public disclosure laws. Implementation tips: • Policies should state who is allowed to authorize the release of videos. • When determining whether to proactively release videos to the public (rather than in response to a public disclosure request), agencies should consider whether the footage will be used in a criminal court case and the potential effects that releasing the data may have on the case. • Policies should clearly state the process for responding to public disclosure requests, including the review and redaction process. • Agencies should always communicate their public disclosure policies to the public.	Public disclosure: pp. 17–19; 33–34; 46–47

Training policies

No.	Recommendation	Findings in Support of Recommendation and Tips for Implementation	Page Reference(s)
26	Body-worn camera training should be required for all agency personnel who may use or otherwise be involved with body-worn cameras.	Personnel who receive training should include the following: • Officers who will be assigned or permitted to wear cameras • Supervisors whose officers wear cameras • Records/evidence management personnel • Training personnel • Internal Affairs • Anyone else who will be involved with the body-worn camera program Implementation tip: • As a courtesy, agencies may wish to offer training to prosecutors so they can better understand how to access the data, what the limitations of the technology are, and how the data may be used in court.	Training: pp. 47–49
27	Before agency personnel are equipped with body-worn cameras, they must receive all mandated training.	This ensures officers are prepared to operate the cameras safely and properly prior to wearing them in the field.	Training: pp. 25; 28–29; 47–49
28	Body-worn camera training should include the following: • All practices and protocols covered by the agency's body-worn camera policy (which should be distributed to all personnel during training) • An overview of relevant state laws governing consent, evidence, privacy, and public disclosure • Procedures for operating the equipment safely and effectively • Scenario-based exercises that replicate situations that officers might encounter in the field • Procedures for downloading and tagging recorded data • Procedures for accessing and reviewing recorded data (only for personnel authorized to access the data) • Procedures for preparing and presenting digital evidence for court • Procedures for documenting and reporting any malfunctioning device or supporting system	Implementation tips: • Agencies can use existing body-worn camera footage to train officers on the proper camera practices and protocols. • Scenario-based training can be useful to help officers become accustomed to wearing and activating their cameras. Some agencies require officers to participate in situational exercise using training model cameras.	Training: pp. 7; 26–30; 47–49
29	A body-worn camera training manual should be created in both digital and hard-copy form and should be readily available at all times to agency personnel.	Implementation tip: • The training manual should be posted on the agency's intranet.	Training: pp. 47–49
30	Agencies should require refresher courses on body-worn camera usage and protocols at least once per year.	Body-worn camera technology is constantly evolving. In addition to yearly refresher courses, training should occur anytime an agency's body-worn camera policy changes. Agencies should also keep abreast of new technology, data storage options, court proceedings, and other issues surrounding body-worn cameras.	Training: pp. 47–49

Policy and program evaluation

No.	Recommendation	Findings in Support of Recommendation and Tips for Implementation	Page Reference(s)
31	Agencies should collect statistical data concerning body-worn camera usage, including when video footage is used in criminal prosecutions and internal affairs matters.	Collecting and releasing data about body-worn cameras helps promote transparency and trust within the community. It also helps agencies to evaluate the effectiveness of their programs, to determine whether their goals are being met, and to identify areas for improvement. Agencies can also use the findings when presenting information about their body-worn camera programs to officers, oversight boards, policymakers, and the community. Implementation tip: • Statistics should be publicly released at various specified points throughout the year or as part of the agency's year-end report.	Engaging the public: pp. 21–22; 24; 28–29; 47–48
32	Agencies should conduct evaluations to analyze the financial impact of implementing a body-worn camera program.	A cost-benefit analysis can help an agency to determine the feasibility of implementing a body-worn camera program. The analysis should examine the following: • The anticipated or actual cost of purchasing equipment, storing recorded data, and responding to public disclosure requests • The anticipated or actual cost savings, including legal fees and other costs associated with defending lawsuits and complaints against officers • Potential funding sources for a body-worn camera program	Financial considerations: pp. 30–34; 48–49 Cost-benefit analysis: p.31 Reducing complaints and lawsuits: pp. 6–9
33	Agencies should conduct periodic reviews of their body-worn camera policies and protocols.	Body-worn camera technology is new and evolving, and the policy issues associated with body-worn cameras are just recently being fully considered. Agencies must continue to examine whether their policies and protocols take into account new technologies, are in compliance with new laws, and reflect the most up-to-date research and best practices. Evaluations will also help agencies determine whether their policies and practices are effective and appropriate for their departments. Implementation tips: • Evaluations should be based on a set of standard criteria and outcome measures. • An initial evaluation should be conducted at the conclusion of the body-worn camera pilot program or at a set period of time (e.g., six months) after the cameras were first implemented. Subsequent evaluations should be conducted on a regular basis as determined by the agency.	Program evaluation: p. 48–49

Additional lessons learned: engaging officers, policymakers, and the community

According to the police officials whom PERF consulted, it is critical for agencies to engage the community, policymakers, courts, oversight boards, unions, frontline officers, and other stakeholders about the department's body-worn camera program. Open communication—both prior to and after camera deployment—can strengthen the perceived legitimacy of the camera program, demonstrate agency transparency, and help educate stakeholders about the realities of using body-worn cameras. The following table presents lessons that agencies shared with PERF with respect to engaging stakeholders.

No.	Lesson Learned	Page Reference(s)
1	Engaging the community prior to implementing a camera program can help secure support for the program and increase the perceived legitimacy of the program within the community.	pp. 21–22; 24
2	Agencies have found it useful to communicate with the public, local policymakers, and other stakeholders about what the cameras will be used for and how the cameras will affect them.	pp. 21–22; 24
3	Social media is an effective way to facilitate public engagement about body-worn cameras.	pp. 21–22; 24
4	Transparency about the agency's camera policies and practices, both prior to and after implementation, can help increase public acceptance and hold agencies accountable. Examples of transparency include posting policies on the agency's website and publicly releasing video recordings of controversial incidents.	pp. 21–22; 24
5	When presenting officers with any new technology, program, or strategy, the best approach includes efforts by agency leaders to engage officers on the topic, explain the goals and benefits of the initiative, and address any concerns officers may have.	pp. 26–27
6	Briefings, roll calls, and meetings with union representatives are effective means to communicate with officers about the agency's body-worn camera program.	pp. 26–27
7	Creating an implementation team that includes representatives from across the agency can help strengthen program legitimacy and ease implementation.	pp. 26–27
8	Agencies have found that officers support a body-worn camera program if they view the cameras as useful tools: e.g., as a technology that helps to reduce complaints and produce evidence that can be used in court or in internal investigations.	pp. 26–27
9	Recruiting an internal "champion" to help inform officers about the benefits of the cameras has proven successful in addressing officers' concerns about embracing the new technology.	pp. 26–27
10	Taking an incremental approach to implementation can help make deployment run more smoothly. This can include testing cameras during a trial period, rolling out cameras slowly, or initially assigning cameras to tech savvy officers.	pp. 26–27
11	Educating oversight bodies about the realities of using cameras can help them to understand operational challenges and why there may be situations in which officers are unable to record. This can include demonstrations to judges, attorneys, and civilian review boards about how the cameras operate.	pp. 28–30

Appendix B. Conference attendees

PERF and the COPS Office convened this one-day conference on September 11, 2013, in Washington, D.C., to discuss the policy and operational issues surrounding body-worn cameras. The titles listed below reflect attendees' positions at the time of the conference.

Albuquerque (NM) Police Department

William Roseman
Deputy Chief of Police

Alexandria (VA) Police Department

David Huchler
Deputy Chief of Police

Eddie Reyes
Deputy Chief of Police

Anne Arundel County (MD) Police Department

Herbert Hasenpusch
Captain

Thomas Kohlmann
Lieutenant

Appleton (WI) Police Department

Gary Lewis
Lieutenant

Arlington County (VA) Police Department

Jason Bryk
Lieutenant

Michael Dunne
Deputy Chief of Police

Lauretta Hill
Assistant Chief of Police

Arnold & Porter LLP

Meredith Esser
Associate

Peter Zimroth
Partner

Atlanta (GA) Police Department

Todd Coyt
Lieutenant

Joseph Spillane
Major

Aurora (CO) Police Department

Dan Mark
Lieutenant

Baltimore County (MD) Police Department

Karen Johnson
Major

James Johnson
Chief of Police

Baltimore (MD) Fraternal Order of Police

Bob Cherry
President

Baltimore (MD) Police Department

Jeronimo Rodriguez
Deputy Police Commissioner

Bay Area Rapid Transit Police Department

Kenton Rainey
Chief of Police

Boyd (VA) Police Department

Michael Brave
Training Officer

Bureau of Justice Assistance
U.S. Department of Justice

David Adams
Senior Policy Advisor

Steve Edwards
Senior Policy Advisor

Kristen Mahoney
Deputy Director of Policy

Denise O'Donnell
Director

Brian Reaves
Senior Statistician

Cornelia Sigworth
Senior Advisor

Christopher Traver
Senior Policy Advisor

Calgary (AB) Police Service

Trevor Daroux
Deputy Chief of Police

Evel Kiez
Sergeant

Asif Rashid
Staff Sergeant

Camden County (NJ) Police Department

Orlando Cuevas
Deputy Chief of Police

**Charlotte-Mecklenburg (NC)
Police Department**

Michael Adams
Major

Stephen Willis
Major

Cincinnati (OH) Police Department

Thomas Streicher
Chief of Police (Retired)

City of Akron (OH) Police Department

James Nice
Chief of Police

Civil Rights Division
U.S. Department of Justice

Roy L. Austin, Jr.
Deputy Assistant Attorney General

Christy Lopez
Deputy Chief

Zazy Lopez
Attorney

Jeffrey Murray
Attorney

Tim Mygatt
Special Counsel

Rashida Ogletree
Attorney

CNA Corporation

James Stewart
Director of Public Safety

Columbus (OH) Division of Police

Gary Cameron
Commander, Narcotics Bureau

**Commission on Accreditation for Law
Enforcement Agencies, Inc.**

Craig Hartley
Deputy Director

CP2, Inc.

Carl Peed
President

Dallas (TX) Police Department

Andrew Acord
Deputy Chief of Police

Dalton (GA) Police Department

Jason Parker
Chief of Police

Daytona Beach (FL) Police Department

Michael Chitwood
Chief of Police

Denver (CO) Police Department

Magen Dodge
Commander

Des Moines (IA) Police Department

Judy Bradshaw
Chief of Police

Todd Dykstra
Captain

Stephen Waymire
Major

Detroit (MI) Police Department

James Craig
Chief of Police

Digital Ally, Inc.

Matthew Andrews
Engineer

Stan Ross
CEO

Eugene (OR) Police Department

James Durr
Captain

Fairfax County (VA) Police Department

Bob Blakley
Lieutenant

Fayetteville (NC) Police Department

Wayne Burgess
Lieutenant

Bradley Chandler
Assistant Chief of Police

Timothy Tew
Lieutenant

Federal Bureau of Investigation

Jacques Battiste
Supervisory Special Agent

Federal Emergency Management Agency

Roberto Hylton
Senior Law Enforcement Advisor

Edward Welch
Director

Fort Collins (CO) Police Department

Cory Christensen
Deputy Chief of Police

Garner (NC) Police Department

Chris Hagwood
Lieutenant

Glenview (IL) Police Department

William Fitzpatrick
Chief of Police

Grand Junction (CO) Police Department

John Camper
Chief of Police

Greater Manchester (UK) Police

Paul Rumney
Detective Chief Superintendent

Greensboro (NC) Police Department

Kenneth Miller
Chief of Police

George Richey
Captain

Wayne Scott
Deputy Chief of Police

Greenville (NC) Police Department

Hassan Aden
Chief of Police

Greenwood & Streicher LLC

Scott Greenwood
CEO

Gulf States Regional Center for Public Safety Innovations

Daphne Levenson
Director

Harrisonburg (VA) Police Department

John Hancock
Officer

Roger Knott
Lieutenant

Hayward (CA) Police Department

Lauren Sugayan
Program Analyst

Henrico County (VA) Division of Police

Douglas Middleton
Chief of Police

Herndon (VA) Police Department

Maggie DeBoard
Chief of Police

Steven Pihonak
Sergeant

Houston (TX) Police Department

Jessica Anderson
Sergeant

James Jones
Captain

Charles McClelland
Chief of Police

Indianapolis (IN) Department of Public Safety

David Riggs
Director

Innovative Management Consulting, Inc.

Thomas Maloney
Senior Consultant

International Association of Chiefs of Police

Mike Fergus
Program Manager

David Roberts
Senior Program Manager

Jersey City (NJ) Police Department

Matthew Dillon
Police ID Officer

Stephen Golecki
Sr. Police ID Officer

Samantha Pescatore
Officer

John Scalcione
Officer

Daniel Sollitti
Captain

L-3 Communications

Michael Burridge
Executive Director, Public Safety

Lakehurst (NJ) Police Department

Eric Higgins
Chief of Police

Lansing (MI) Police Department

Michael Yankowski
Chief of Police

Las Vegas Metropolitan (NV) Police Department

Liesl Freedman
General Counsel

Thomas Roberts
Captain

Leesburg (VA) Police Department

Carl Maupin
Lieutenant

Lenexa (KS) Police Department

Dawn Layman
Major

Los Angeles County Sheriff's Department

David Betkey
Division Chief

Kevin Goran
Division Chief

James Hellmold
Assistant Sheriff

Chris Marks
Lieutenant

Los Angeles Police Department

Greg Meyer
Captain (Retired)

Louisville (KY) Metro Police Department

Robert Schroeder
Major

Lynchburg (VA) Police Department

Mark Jamison
Captain

Ryan Zuidema
Captain

Madison (WI) Police Department

June Groehler
Lieutenant

Manning & Kass, Ellrod, Ramirez, Trester

Mildred Olinn
Partner

Eugene Ramirez
Senior Partner

Maryland State Police Department

Michael Brady
Sergeant

Clifford Hughes
Assistant Bureau Chief

Thomas Vondersmith
Director

Meriden (CT) Police Department

Jeffry Cossette
Chief of Police

Timothy Topulos
Deputy Chief of Police

Mesa (AZ) Police Department

Tony Filler
Commander

Metropolitan Nashville (TN) Police Department

Michael Anderson
Chief of Police

John Singleton
IT Security Manager

Metropolitan (DC) Police Department

Brian Bobick
Sergeant

Alfred Durham
Assistant Chief of Police

Barry Gersten
CIO

Lamar Greene
Assistant Chief of Police

Cathy Lanier
Chief of Police

Thomas Wilkins
Executive Director

Miami Beach (FL) Police Department

David De La Espriella
Captain

Milwaukee (WI) Police Department

Mary Hoerig
Inspector of Police

Minneapolis (MN) Police Department

Bruce Folkens
Commander

Janeé Harteau
Chief of Police

Montgomery County (MD) Police Department

Brian Acken
Director

Luther Reynolds
Assistant Chief of Police

Motorola Solutions, Inc.

Domingo Herraiz
Vice President

Kelly Kirwan
Corporate Vice President

Steve Sebestyen
Business Development Manager

MPH Industries Inc.

Larry Abel
Senior Training Officer

National Institute of Justice
U.S. Department of Justice

Brett Chapman
Social Science Analyst

William Ford
Division Director

National Law Enforcement Museum

Sarah Haggerty
Associate Curator

National Press Photographers Association

Mickey Osterreicher
General Counsel

New Haven (CT) Police Department

Luiz Casanova
Assistant Chief of Police

New Orleans (LA) Police Department

Ronal Serpas
Superintendent of Police

New South Wales (AUS) Police Force

Stephen Cullen
Chief Superintendent

New York City Police Department

Terrence Riley
Inspector

Newark (NJ) Police Department

Sheilah Coley
Chief of Police

Samuel DeMaio
Director

Michele MacPhee
Lieutenant

Brian O'Hara
Lieutenant

Norfolk (VA) Police Department

Frances Emerson
Captain

James Ipock
Lieutenant

Northern California Regional Intelligence Center

Daniel Mahoney
Deputy Director

Oakland (CA) Police Department

Sean Whent
Chief of Police

Office of Community Oriented Policing Services
U.S. Department of Justice

Melissa Bradley
Program Specialist

Helene Bushwick
Supervisory Policy Analyst

Joshua Ederheimer
Acting Director

Mora Fiedler
Social Science Analyst

Dean Kueter
Acting Chief of Staff

Debra McCullough
Senior Social Science Analyst

Katherine McQuay
Senior Policy Analyst

Tawana Waugh
Senior Program Specialist

John Wells
Program Specialist

Office of Justice Programs
U.S. Department of Justice

Linda Mansour
Intergovernmental Affairs

Katherine Darke Schmitt
Policy Advisor

Panasonic

Norihiro Kondo
Group Manager

Philadelphia (PA) Police Department

Charles Ramsey
Police Commissioner

Anthony Washington
Inspector

Phoenix (AZ) Police Department

Dave Harvey
Assistant Chief of Police

Police and Public Safety Consultant

Robert Lunney
Consultant

Police Foundation

Jim Bueermann
President

Jim Specht
Assistant to the President for Communications and Policy

Poulsbo (WA) Police Department

Alan Townsend
Chief of Police

Prince George's County (MD) Police Department

Joshua Brackett
Corporal

Mark Person
Major

Henry Stawinski III
Deputy Chief of Police

Hector Velez
Deputy Chief of Police

Prince William County (VA) Police Department

Charlie Deane
Chief of Police (Retired)

Javid Elahi
Lieutenant

Thomas Pulaski
Senior Administrative Manager

Ramsey County (MN) Sheriff's Office

Robert Allen
Director of Planning and Policy Analysis

Rialto (CA) Police Department

William Farrar
Chief of Police

Richmond (CA) Police Department

Allwyn Brown
Deputy Chief of Police

Richmond (VA) Police Department

Scott Booth
Major

Sydney Collier
Major

Roger Russell
Captain

Riverside (CA) Police Department

Bruce Loftus
Lieutenant

Roanoke (VA) County Police Department

Mike Warner
Assistant Chief of Police

Robinson & Yu LLC

David Robinson
Principal

Royal Canadian Mounted Police

K. Troy Lightfoot
Director of Operational Policy and Compliance

San Diego County District Attorney, Bureau of Investigations

Adolfo Gonzales
Chief Investigator

San Leandro (CA) Police Department

Sandra Spagnoli
Chief of Police

Seattle (WA) Police Department

David Puente
Detective

Spokane (WA) Police Department

Bradley Arleth
Commander

Craig Meidl
Assistant Chief of Police

Tim Schwering
Deputy Director

Springfield (MO) Police Department

Paul Williams
Chief of Police

Tampa (FL) Police Department

Michael Baumaister
Captain

TASER International

Jeff Kukowski
Chief Operating Officer

Tennessee Association of Chiefs of Police

Maggi McLean Duncan
Executive Director and CEO

Thomasville (NC) Police Department

Rusty Fritz
Sergeant

Topeka (KS) Police Department

Ronald Miller
Chief of Police

Toronto (ON) Police Service

Mike Federico
Deputy Chief of Police

John Sandeman
Unit Commander

Peter Sloly
Deputy Chief of Police

Tucson (AZ) Police Department

Sharon Allen
Deputy Chief of Police

Jim Rizzi
Captain

UCLA Anderson School of Management

Peter Scranton

**University of California,
San Diego Police Department**

Orville King
Chief of Police

David Rose
Captain

University of South Florida

Lorie Fridell
Associate Professor

U.S. Capitol Police Department

Kim Dine
Chief of Police

Daniel Malloy
Inspector

U.S. State Department

Jody Platt
Public Diplomacy Officer

VIEVU

Steven Lovell
President

Virginia Beach Police Department

James Cervera
Chief of Police

Richard Cheatham
PTO Coordinator

Todd Jones
Lieutenant

West Palm Beach (FL) Police Department

Anthony Kalil
Captain

Sarah Mooney
Captain

Yakima (WA) Police Department

Jeff Schneider
Captain

About PERF

The **Police Executive Research Forum** (PERF) is an independent research organization that focuses on critical issues in policing. Since its founding in 1976, PERF has identified best practices on fundamental issues such as reducing police use of force, developing community policing and problem-oriented policing, using technologies to deliver police services to the community, and evaluating crime reduction strategies.

PERF strives to advance professionalism in policing and to improve the delivery of police services through the exercise of strong national leadership, public debate of police and criminal justice issues, and research and policy development.

In addition to conducting research and publishing reports on our findings, PERF conducts management studies of individual law enforcement agencies, educates hundreds of police officials each year in a three-week executive development program, and provides executive search services to governments that wish to conduct national searches for their next police chief.

All of PERF's work benefits from PERF's status as a membership organization of police officials, academics, federal government leaders, and others with an interest in policing and criminal justice.

All PERF members must have a four-year college degree and must subscribe to a set of founding principles, emphasizing the importance of research and public debate in policing, adherence to the Constitution and the highest standards of ethics and integrity, and accountability to the communities that police agencies serve.

PERF is governed by a member-elected president and board of directors and a board-appointed executive director. A staff of approximately 30 full-time professionals is based in Washington, D.C.

To learn more, visit PERF online at www.policeforum.org.

About the COPS Office

The **Office of Community Oriented Policing Services (COPS Office)** is the component of the U.S. Department of Justice responsible for advancing the practice of community policing by the nation's state, local, territory, and tribal law enforcement agencies through information and grant resources.

Community policing is a philosophy that promotes organizational strategies that support the systematic use of partnerships and problem-solving techniques, to proactively address the immediate conditions that give rise to public safety issues such as crime, social disorder, and fear of crime.

Rather than simply responding to crimes once they have been committed, community policing concentrates on preventing crime and eliminating the atmosphere of fear it creates. Earning the trust of the community and making those individuals stakeholders in their own safety enables law enforcement to better understand and address both the needs of the community and the factors that contribute to crime.

The COPS Office awards grants to state, local, territory, and tribal law enforcement agencies to hire and train community policing professionals, acquire and deploy cutting-edge crime fighting technologies, and develop and test innovative policing strategies. COPS Office funding also provides training and technical assistance to community members and local government leaders and all levels of law enforcement. The COPS Office has produced and compiled a broad range of information resources that can help law enforcement better address specific crime and operational issues, and help community leaders better understand how to work cooperatively with their law enforcement agency to reduce crime.

- Since 1994, the COPS Office has invested more than $14 billion to add community policing officers to the nation's streets, enhance crime fighting technology, support crime prevention initiatives, and provide training and technical assistance to help advance community policing.

- To date, the COPS Office has funded approximately 125,000 additional officers to more than 13,000 of the nation's 18,000 law enforcement agencies across the country in small and large jurisdictions alike.

- Nearly 700,000 law enforcement personnel, community members, and government leaders have been trained through COPS Office-funded training organizations.

- To date, the COPS Office has distributed more than 8.57 million topic-specific publications, training curricula, white papers, and resource CDs.

COPS Office resources, covering a wide breadth of community policing topics—from school and campus safety to gang violence—are available, at no cost, through its online Resource Center at www.cops.usdoj.gov. This easy-to-navigate website is also the grant application portal, providing access to online application forms.

www.ingramcontent.com/pod-product-compliance
Lightning Source LLC
Chambersburg PA
CBHW080322290526
45790CB00005B/2149